The Old North State Fact Book

The Old North State Fact Book

Office of Archives and History
North Carolina Department of Cultural Resources
Raleigh
2008

Printed by Jostens, Inc.

CONTENTS

OTHER OFFICIAL ADOPTIONS

GOVERNORS

FOREWORD

The *North Carolina Manual*, issued biennially by the Office of the Secretary of State, includes an introductory chapter giving information on the state's history, the State Capitol, state flag, seal, flower, bird, and other similar topics. Because the Historical Publications Section of the Office of Archives and History, North Carolina Department of Cultural Resources, frequently receives requests for such information from curious schoolchildren and interested citizens, an arrangement was made a number of years ago to publish portions of the first part of the *Manual* as a separate booklet under the title, *The Old North State Fact Book*.

This revision contains more color images than previous editions, as well as more text. It has also been indexed. Special thanks go to Denise Craig and Susan Trimble for their diligent work in updating the text and the images.

Donna E. Kelly, *Administrator*
Historical Publications Section

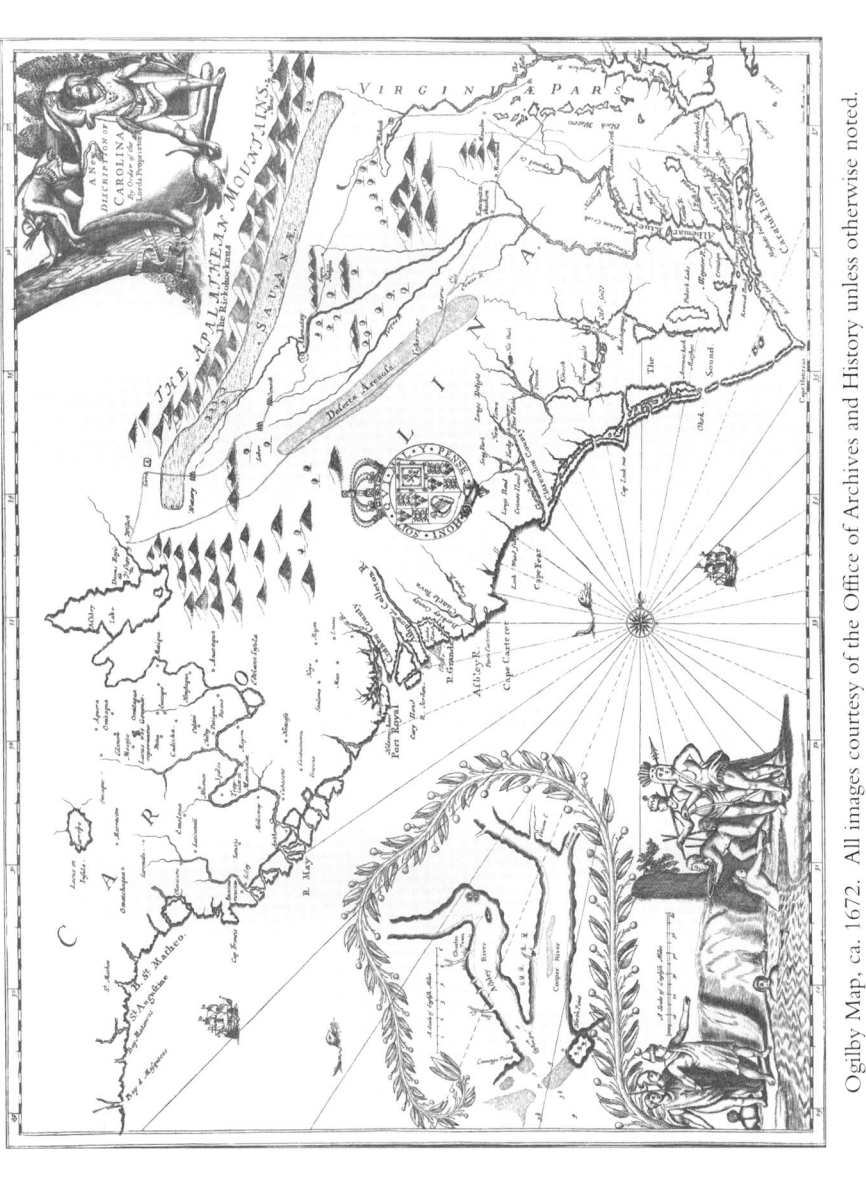

Ogilby Map, ca. 1672. All images courtesy of the Office of Archives and History unless otherwise noted.

AN EARLY HISTORY OF NORTH CAROLINA

The first known European exploration of North Carolina occurred during the summer of 1524. A Florentine navigator named Giovanni da Verrazano, in the service of France, explored the coastal area of North Carolina between the Cape Fear River area and Kitty Hawk. A report of his findings was sent to Francis I, and published in Richard Hakluyt's *Divers Voyages touching the Discoverie of America*. No attempt was made to colonize the area. Between 1540 and 1570, several Spanish explorers from the Florida Gulf region explored portions of North Carolina, but again, no permanent settlements were established.

Coastal North Carolina was the scene of the first attempt to colonize America by English-speaking people. Two colonies were begun in the 1580s under a charter granted by Queen Elizabeth to Sir Walter Raleigh (sometimes spelled "Ralegh"). The first colony, established in 1585 under the leadership of Ralph Lane, ended in failure. A second expedition under the leadership of John White began in the spring of

Sir Walter Raleigh

1587 when 110 settlers, including seventeen women and nine children, set sail for the New World. The White Colony arrived near Hatteras in June 1587, and went on to Roanoke Island, where they found the houses built by Ralph Lanes's expedition still standing. Two significant events occurred shortly after the colonists' arrival—two "friendly" Indians were baptized, and a child was born. Virginia Dare, as the baby was named, was the first child born to English-speaking parents in the New World.

The colonists faced many problems. As supplies ran short, White was pressured to return to England for provisions. Once in England, White was unable to immediately return to Roanoke because of an impending attack by the Spanish Armada. When he was finally able to return in 1590, he found only the remnants of what was once a

This engraving, made in the nineteenth century, represents John White at the time of his return to Roanoke Island in 1590. Reproduced from *The Lost Colonists: Their Fortune and Probable Fate*.

thriving settlement. There were no signs of life, only the letters "CRO" carved on a tree, and the word "CROATOAN" carved on another tree near the entrance to the colonists' fort. Much speculation has been made about the fate of the "Lost Colony," but no one has successfully explained the disappearance of the colony and its settlers.

The first permanent English settlers in North Carolina emigrated from the tidewater area of southeastern Virginia. The first of these "overflow" settlers moved into the Albemarle area of northeast North Carolina around 1650.

In 1663, Charles II granted a charter to eight English gentlemen who had helped him regain the throne of England. The charter document contains the following description of the territory that the eight Lords Proprietors were granted title to:

> All that Territory or Tract of ground, situate, lying, and being within our Dominions in America, extending from the North end of the Island called Luck Island, which lies in the Southern Virginia Seas and within six and Thirty Degrees of the Northern Latitude, and to the West as far as the South Seas; and so Southerly as far as the River Saint Mathias, which borders upon the Coast of Florida, and within one and Thirty Degrees of Northern Latitude; and West in a direct Line as far as the South Seas aforesaid; Together with all and singular Ports, Harbours, Bays, Rivers, Isles, and Islets belonging unto the Country aforesaid; And also, all the Soil, Lands, Fields, Woods, Mountains, Farms, Lakes, Rivers, Bays, and Islets situate or being within the Bounds or Limits aforesaid; with the Fishing of all sorts of Fish, Whales, Sturgeons, and all other Royal Fishes in the Sea, Bays, Islets, and Rivers within the premises, and the Fish therein taken;

NAME OF STATE AND NICKNAMES

In 1629, King Charles I of England "erected into a province," all the land from Albemarle Sound (in present-day North Carolina) on the north to the St. John's River (in present-day Florida) on the south, which he directed should be called "Carolana." Charles II renamed the province "Carolina," which is from the word Carolus, the Latin form of Charles. When Carolina divided in 1710, the southern part was called South Carolina and the northern, or older settlement, North Carolina. From this came the nickname the "Old North State."

The state's more famous nickname, "The Tar Heel State," emerged during the Civil War. Historians have recorded that the principal products during the early history of North Carolina were tar, pitch, and turpentine. It was during one of the fiercest battles of the Civil War, so the story goes, that the column supporting the North Carolina troops was driven from the field. After the battle, the North Carolinians, who had successfully fought it out alone, were greeted from the passing derelict regiment with the question: "Any more tar down in the Old North State, boys?" Quick as a flash came the answer: "No, not a bit, old Jeff's bought it all up." "Is that so; what is he going to do with it?" was asked. "He is going to put it on you-uns heels to make you stick better in the next fight." Historian R. B. Creecy relates that General Robert E. Lee, upon hearing of the incident, said, "God bless the Tar Heel boys," and from that they took the name. (Adapted from *Grandfather Tales of North Carolina* by R. B. Creecy and *Histories of North Carolina Regiments*, Vol. III, by Walter Clark. See also Michael W. Taylor's *Tar Heels: How North Carolinians Got Their Nickname*.)

And moreover, all Veins, Mines, and Quarries, as well discovered as not discovered, of Gold, Silver, Gems, and precious Stones, and all other, whatsoever be it, of Stones, Metals, or any other thing whatsoever found or to be found within the Country, Isles, and Limits aforesaid. . . .

The territory was to be called "Carolina" in honor of Charles I. In 1665, a second charter was granted in order to clarify territorial

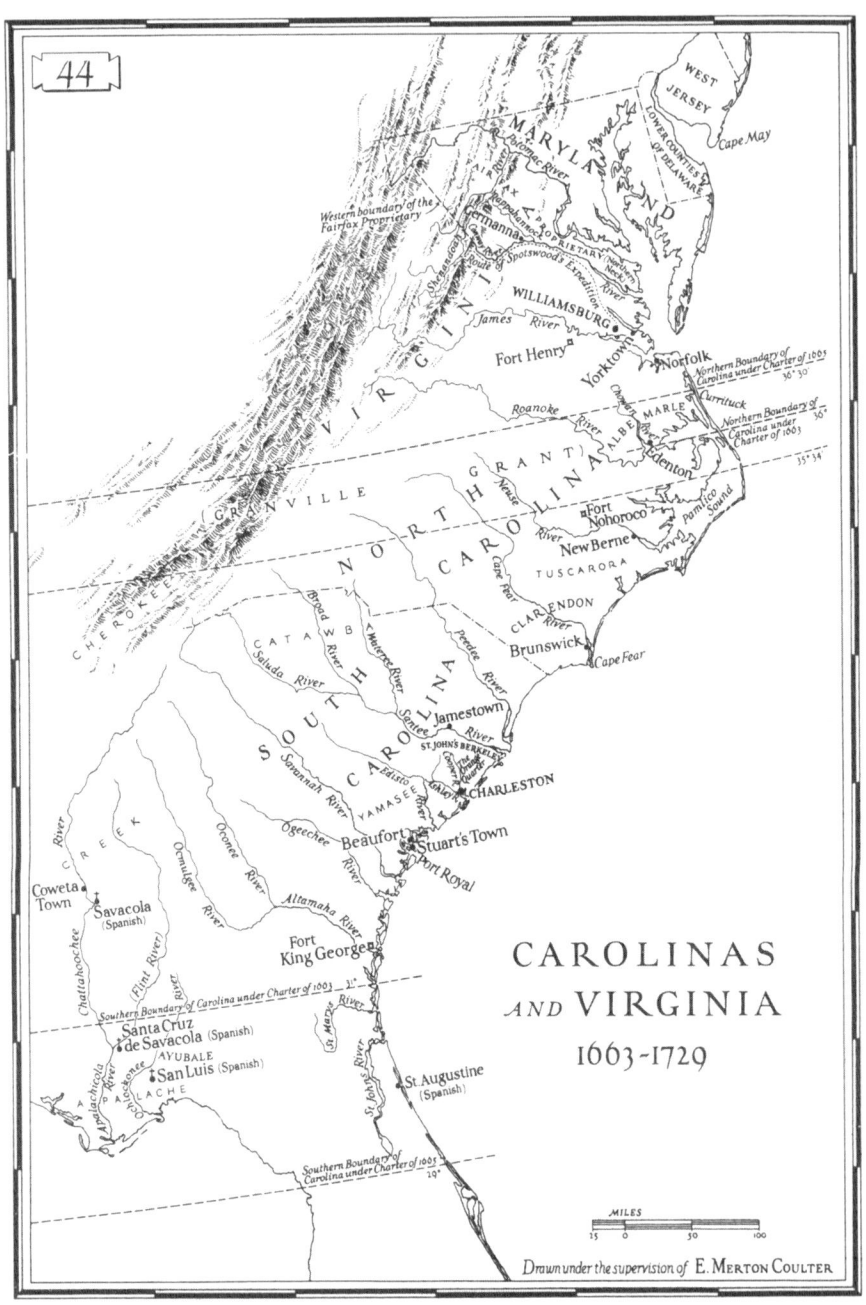

Map depicting the northern and southern boundaries of Carolina under the Charters of 1663 and 1665, and the Granville Grant. Plate 44, from *Atlas of American History, Revised Edition*, by Kenneth T. Jackson and James Truslow Adams, eds., Charles Scribner's Sons, (c) 1978, Charles Scribners. Reprinted by permission of The Gale Group.

questions not answered in the first charter. This charter extended the boundary lines of Carolina to include:

> All that Province, Territory, or Tract of ground, situate, lying, and being within our Dominions of America aforesaid, extending North and Eastward as far as the North end of Carahtuke River or Gullet; upon a straight westerly line to Wyonoake Creek, which lies within or about the degrees of thirty six and thirty Minutes, Northern latitude, and so West in a direct line as far as the South Seas; and South and Westward as far as the degrees of twenty nine, inclusive, northern latitude; and so West in a direct line as far as the south Seas.

Between 1663 and 1729, North Carolina was under the control of the Lords Proprietors and their descendants who commissioned colonial officials and authorized the governor and his council to grant lands in the name of the Lords Proprietors. In 1669, the Lords Proprietors adopted the Fundamental Constitutions of Carolina as a model for the government of Carolina. Albemarle County was divided into local governmental units called precincts. Initially there were three precincts—Berkley, Carteret, and Shaftesbury—but as the colony expanded to the south and west, new precincts were created. By 1729, there was a total of eleven precincts—six in Albemarle County and five in Bath County, which had been created in 1696. Although the Albemarle region was the first permanent settlement in the Carolina area, another populated region soon developed around present-day Charleston, South Carolina. Because of the natural harbor and easier access to trade with the West Indies, more attention was given to developing the Charleston area than her northern counterparts. For a twenty-year period, 1692-1712, the colonies of North and South Carolina existed as one unit of government. Although North Carolina still had her own assembly and council, the governor of Carolina resided in Charleston, and a deputy governor was appointed for North Carolina.

In 1729, seven of the Lords Proprietors sold their interest in North Carolina to the Crown, and North Carolina became a royal colony. The eighth proprietor, Lord Granville, retained economic interest and continued granting land in the northern half of North Carolina.

The Crown supervised all political and administrative functions in the colony until 1775.

Colonial government in North Carolina changed little between the proprietary and royal periods, the only major difference being who appointed colonial officials. There were two primary units of government: the governor and his council and a colonial assembly whose representatives were elected by the qualified voters of the county. Colonial courts, unlike today's courts, rarely involved themselves in formulating governmental policy. All colonial officials were appointed by either the Lords Proprietors prior to 1729, or by the Crown afterwards. Members of the colonial assembly were elected from the various precincts (counties) and from certain towns that had been granted representation. The term "precinct" as a geographical unit ceased to exist after 1735. These areas became known as "counties," and about the same time "Albemarle County" and "Bath County" ceased to exist as governmental units.

The governor was an appointed official, as were the colonial secretary, attorney general, surveyor general, and the receiver general. All officials served at the pleasure of the Lords Proprietors or the Crown. During the proprietary period, the council was comprised of appointed persons who were to look after the proprietors' interests in the New World. The council served as an advisory group to the governor during the proprietary and royal periods, and also served as the upper house of the legislature when the assembly was in session. When vacancies occurred in colonial offices or on the council, the governor was authorized to carry out all mandates of the proprietors, and could make a temporary appointment until the vacancy could be filled by proprietary or royal commission. One member of the council was chosen president of the group, and many council members were also colonial officials. If a governor or deputy governor was unable to carry on as chief executive because of illness, death, resignation, or absence from the colony, the president of the council became the chief executive and exercised all powers of the governor until the governor returned or a new governor was commissioned.

The colonial assembly was made up of men elected from each precinct and town where representation had been granted. Not all counties were entitled to the same number of representatives. Many of the older counties had five representatives each, while those formed after 1696 were each allowed only two. Each town granted representation was allowed one representative. The presiding officer of the colonial assembly was called the speaker and was elected from the entire membership of the house. When a vacancy occurred, a new election was ordered by the speaker to fill it. On the final day of each session, the bills passed by the legislature were signed by both the speaker and the president of the council.

The colonial assembly could meet only when called into session by the governor. Being the only body authorized to grant the governor's salary or to be responsible for spending tax monies, the legislature met on a regular basis until just before the Revolutionary War. However, there was a constant battle for authority between the governor and his council on the one hand and the general assembly on the other. Two of the most explosive issues involved fiscal control of the colony's revenues and the election of treasurers, both privileges of the assembly. Another issue was who had the authority to create new counties. On more than one occasion, elected representatives from counties created by the governor and council, without consultation and proper legislative action by the lower house, were refused seats until the matter was resolved. These conflicts between the executive and legislative bodies were to have a profound effect on the organization of the state government after independence.

North Carolina, on April 12, 1776, authorized her delegates to the Continental Congress to vote for independence. This was the first official action by a colony calling for independence. The eighty-three delegates present in Halifax at the Fourth Provincial Congress unanimously adopted the Halifax Resolves, which read as follows:

> The Select Committee to take into Consideration the Usurpations and Violences attempted and Committed by the King and Parliament of Britain against America, and the further Measures to be taken for frustrating the Same, and for the better defence of this province, reported as follows, to wit.
>
> It appears to your Committee, that pursuant to the plan concerted by the British Ministry for subjugating America, the King and

Joseph Hewes

North Carolina Signers of the Declaration of Independence

William Hooper

John Penn

Parliament of Great Britain have usurped a power over the persons and properties of the people unlimited and uncontrouled. And disregarding their humble petitions for peace, Liberty and Safety, have made divers Legislative Acts, denouncing War, Famine and every Species of Calamity, against the Continent in General.

That British Fleet and Armies have been and still are daily employed in destroying the people, and committing the most horrid devastations on the Country.

That Governors in different Colonies have declared Protection to Slaves who should imbrue their hands in the blood of their masters.

That the Ships belonging to America are declared prizes of War, and many of them have been Violently Seized and Confiscated.

In consequence of all which, multitudes of the people have been destroyed, or from easy Circumstances reduced to the most lamentable distress.

And whereas the moderation hitherto manifested by the united Colonies, and their sincere desire to be reconciled to the Mother Country on Constitutional principles, have procured no mitigation of the aforesaid Wrongs and Usurpations, and no hopes remain of obtaining redress, by those means alone which have been hitherto tried, your Committee are of Opinion that the House should enter into the following resolve,

Resolved that the Delegates for this Colony in the Continental Congress be impowered to Concur with the Delegates of the other Colonies in declaring Independency and forming foreign Alliances, reserving to this Colony, the Sole and Exclusive right of forming a Constitution and Laws for this Colony, and of appointing Delegates from time to time (under the direction of a General representation thereof) to meet the Delegates of the other Colonies for Such purposes as shall be hereafter pointed out.

The Halifax Resolves were important not only because they were the first official action calling for independence, but also because they were not a unilateral recommendation. They were instead recommendations directed to all the colonies and their delegates assembled at the Continental Congress in Philadelphia. Virginia followed with her own recommendations soon after the adoption of the Halifax Resolves and on July 4, the final draft of the Declaration of Independence was signed. William Hooper, Joseph Hewes, and John Penn were the delegates from North Carolina who signed the Declaration of Independence.

Tryon Palace, New Bern. Photograph courtesy of Tryon Palace Historic Sites & Gardens.

In early December 1776, delegates to the Fifth Provincial Congress adopted the first constitution for North Carolina. On December 21, 1776, Richard Caswell became the first governor of North Carolina under the new constitution. On November 21, 1789, the state adopted the United States Constitution, becoming the twelfth state to enter the Federal Union. In 1788, North Carolina had rejected the Constitution because it lacked the necessary amendments to ensure freedom of the people. The Bill of Rights satisfied the concerns of antifederalists enough to ensure the state's adoption of the Constitution a year later.

A Constitutional Convention was held in 1835 and among several changes made in the constitution was the method of electing the governor. After this change, the governor was elected by the people for a term of two years instead of being elected by the legislature for one year. Edward Bishop Dudley was the first governor elected by the people.

In 1868, a second constitution, which drastically altered North Carolina government, was adopted. For the first time, all major state officers were elected by the people. The governor and other executive officers were elected to four-year terms, while the justices of the supreme court and judges of the superior court were elected to eight-year terms. The members of the General Assembly continued to be elected for two-year terms. Between 1868 and 1970, numerous amendments were incorporated into the 1868 constitution, so that in

The Maude Moore Latham Memorial Garden at Tryon Palace. Photograph courtesy of Tryon Palace Historic Sites & Gardens.

1970, the people voted to adopt a completely new constitution. Since then, several amendments have been ratified, but one in particular is a break from the past. In 1977, the people voted to allow the governor and lieutenant governor to run for reelection successively for an additional term.

North Carolina has had two permanent capitals—New Bern and Raleigh—and there have been three capitols. Tryon Palace in New Bern was constructed between 1767 and 1770 by royal governor William Tryon, and the main building was destroyed by fire on February 27, 1798. The palace was reconstructed, and new gardens were established in the 1950s when the complex opened as a historic site. The first Capitol in Raleigh was occupied in 1794 and was destroyed by fire on June 21, 1831. The present Capitol was completed in 1840.

In 1790, North Carolina ceded her western lands, which included Davidson, Greene, Hawkins, Sullivan, Sumner, Tennessee, and Washington counties, to the federal government. Between 1790 and 1796, the territory was known as Tennessee Territory, but in 1796 it became simply Tennessee, the fifteenth state in the Union.

The State Capitol in Raleigh, North Carolina.

THE STATE CAPITOL

The North Carolina State Capitol is one of the finest and best-preserved examples of a major civic building in the Greek Revival style of architecture.

Prior to 1792, North Carolina legislators met in various towns throughout the state, gathering most frequently in Halifax, Hillsborough, and New Bern. Meetings were held in local plantation houses, courthouses, and even churches. However, when the city of Raleigh was established as the permanent seat of the government of North Carolina in 1792, a simple, two-story brick State House was built on Union Square. The State House hosted its first session in 1794, and construction was fully completed in 1796.

The State House was enlarged between 1820 and 1824 by state architect William Nichols, who added a third floor, eastern and western wings, and a domed rotunda at the building's center. The rotunda housed a statue of President George Washington by sculptor Antonio Canova, acquired by the state in 1821. When the State House burned down on June 21, 1831, the statue was damaged beyond repair.

The General Assembly of 1832-1833 ordered that a new Capitol be built as an enlarged version of the old State House. The new Capitol would be a cross-shaped building with a central, domed rotunda. The sum of $50,000 was appropriated, and a building commission appointed to initiate the plan. The Commissioners for Rebuilding the Capitol first employed both Nichols and his son, William Nichols Jr., to help them prepare plans for the building. In August of 1833, after delivering the plans, they were replaced by the distinguished New York architects Ithiel Town and Alexander Jackson Davis. Town and Davis greatly improved upon the earlier design and developed a plan giving the Capitol its present appearance.

David Paton (1802-1882), an architect born in Edinburgh, Scotland, and who had worked for the noted English architect Sir John Soane, was hired in September 1834 to superintend the construction of the Capitol. Paton replaced Town and Davis as the Commissioners' architect in early 1835. The Capitol was completed under Paton's supervision except for the exterior stone walls that were largely in place when he arrived in Raleigh.

Paton made several modifications to the Town and Davis plans for the interior. Among the changes were the cantilevered gallery at the second-floor level of the rotunda, the groined masonry vaulting of the first-floor offices and corridor ceilings, and the interior arrangement of the east and west porticoes.

After clearing away the debris from the old State House, excavations were made, and a new foundation was laid. The cornerstone was set in place on July 4, 1833. After the initial foundation was laid, work progressed slowly, and the original appropriation was soon exhausted. At the next session of the General Assembly, an additional appropriation of $75,000 was made to continue construction. Many skilled immigrant Scottish artisans came to Raleigh and were involved in this phase of construction.

The Capitol was completed in 1840 at a total cost (including furnishings) of $532,682.34, or more than three times the yearly general revenues of the state at that time.

Architect David Paton gave the following description of the new edifice:

> The State Capitol is 160 feet in length from north to south by 140 feet from east to west. The whole height is 97½ feet in the center. The apex of pediment is 64 feet in height. The stylobate is 18 feet in height. The columns of the east and west porticoes are 5 feet 2½ inches in diameter. An entablature, including blocking course, is continued around the building 12 feet high.
>
> The columns and entablature are Grecian Doric, and copied from the Temple of Minerva, commonly called the Parthenon, which was erected in Athens about 500 years before Christ. An octagon tower surrounds the rotunda, which is ornamented with Grecian cornices, etc., and its dome is decorated at top with a similar ornament to that of the Choragic Monument of Lysicrates, commonly called the Lanthorn of Demosthenes.
>
> The interior of the Capitol is divided into three stories: First, the lower story, consisting of ten rooms, eight of which are appropriated as offices to the Governor, Secretary, Treasurer, and Comptroller, each having two rooms of the same size—the one containing an area of 649 square feet and four closets, the other 528 square feet—two committee rooms, each containing 200 square feet and four closets: also the rotunda, corridors, vestibules, and piazzas, contain an area of 4,370 square feet. The vestibules are decorated with columns and

antae, similar to those of the Ionic Temple on the Ilissus, near the Acropolis of Athens. The remainder is groined with stone and brick, springing from columns and pilasters of the Roman Doric.

The second story consists of Senatorial and Representatives' chambers, the former containing an area of 2,545 and the latter 2,849 square feet. Four apartments enter from the Senate Chamber, two of which contain each an area of 169 square feet, and the other two contain each an area of 154 square feet; also, two rooms enter from Representatives' chamber, each containing an area of 170 square feet; of two committee rooms, each containing an area of 231 square feet; of four presses and the passages, stairs, lobbies, and colonnades, containing an area of 3,204 square feet.

The lobbies and Hall of Representatives have their columns and antae of the Octagon Tower of Andronicus Cyrrhestes and the plan of the hall is of the formation of the Greek theatre and the columns and antae in the Senatorial chamber and rotunda are of the Temple of Erectheus, Minerva, Polias, and Pandrosus, in the Acropolis of Athens, near the above named Parthenon.

The third, or attic story, consists of rooms appropriated to the Supreme Court and Library, each containing an area of 693 square feet. Galleries of both houses have an area of 1,300 square feet; also two apartments entering from Senate gallery, each 169 square feet; of four presses and the lobbies' stairs, 988 square feet. These lobbies as well as rotunda, are lit with cupolas, and it is proposed to finish the court and library in the florid Gothic style.

Most of the Capitol's architectural details, including the columns, mouldings, ornamental plasterwork, and ornamental honeysuckle atop the dome, were carefully patterned after features of Greek temples: the exterior columns are Doric in order and are modeled after those of the Parthenon; the chamber of the House of Representatives follows the semi-circular plan of a Greek amphitheatre, and its architectural ornamentation is in the Corinthian order of the Tower of the Winds; and the Senate Chamber is decorated in the Ionic order of the Erechtheum. The only non-classical parts of the building are two large rooms on the third floor that were finished in the Gothic style that was just beginning its popularity in American architectural circles.

The ornamental ironwork, plasterwork, chandeliers, hardware, and marble mantels of the Capitol came from Philadelphia. The desks and chairs in the House and Senate Chambers were made by Raleigh cabinetmaker, William Thompson.

Stairways in the east and west porticoes give access to the second floor, where the Senate and House Chambers and related offices are located. Rooms in the east and west wings, originally designated as legislative committee rooms, now serve other purposes. On the third floor are the galleries of the Senate and House Chambers, and in the east and west wings are the original State Supreme Court Chamber and State Library room. Both are decorated in the Gothic style. The domed, top-lit vestibules of these two rooms are especially noteworthy and based on designs by Soane.

In 1970, the state acquired a duplicate of the original marble statue of Washington by Canova that is now located in the rotunda of the Capitol. In niches around the rotunda are busts of three North Carolina governors—John M. Morehead, William A. Graham, and Samuel Johnston—and United States senator Matthew W. Ransom.

Although the Capitol housed all of state government until the late 1880s, today the only official occupants of the Capitol are the governor and his staff, who maintain offices throughout the first floor. The state supreme court moved to its own building in 1888, and in 1963, the General Assembly moved into the newly constructed Legislative Building. This was the first building erected by the state exclusively for use by the General Assembly.

THE CAPITOL TODAY

The Capitol has changed less in appearance than any major American civic building of its era. The stonework, the ornamental plaster and ironwork, the furniture of the legislative chambers, and all but one of the marble mantels that visitors see today are original, not restorations or reproductions. Yet, continuous and heavy use since 1840 has left its mark on the building, and to cope with this wear and tear, the Capitol receives periodic attention. Rehabilitation work began in 1971 with the intention of preserving and enhancing the architectural splendor and decorative beauty of the Capitol for future generations. Work done included replacing the leaky copper roof, cleaning and sealing the exterior stone, and repainting the rotunda. More recently, plasterwork damaged by roof leaks was repaired, obsolete wiring and plumbing were replaced, the heating and cooling systems in the upper floors were reworked to make them less conspicuous, worn carpets and draperies were replaced, and the rest of the interior was repainted.

As our nation celebrated its bicentennial in 1976, our State Capitol was enjoying a celebration of its own. Several years of renovation work to the old Senate and House chambers and the executive offices on the first floor were completed, and the Capitol was once again ready to receive occupants. Governor James B. Hunt Jr. and some of his staff moved back in, as did longtime resident, Secretary of State Thad Eure. Mr. Eure served in the Capitol longer than anyone in its history— sixty years as of his retirement in early 1989. Occupying the Capitol at the time of this writing are Gov. Michael F. Easley and his staff, who maintain offices on the first floor.

In late 1988 and early 1989, extensive landscape and grounds renovations were begun to enhance the beauty

George Washington statue in the Capitol rotunda.

of the Capitol and to improve its visibility. In an effort to make the Capitol more accessible to the people of North Carolina, the building has been opened to the public on weekends with guided tours available.

THE LEGISLATIVE BUILDING

In 1959, the General Assembly appropriated funds for the construction of a new legislative building. The new facility was needed to accommodate a growing legislative branch and to provide larger quarters for legislators and staff. The act creating the building commission was passed on June 12, 1959. The commission was made

The Legislative Building in Raleigh, North Carolina.

up of seven people—two who had served in the state senate to be appointed by the president of the senate, two who had served in the state house of representatives to be appointed by the Speaker of the House, and three appointed by the governor. Lt. Gov. Luther E. Barnhardt, president of the senate, appointed Archie K. Davis and Robert F. Morgan. Speaker of the House Addison Hewlett appointed B. I. Satterfield and Thomas J. White. Gov. Luther Hodges appointed A. E. Finley, Edwin Gill, and Oliver Rowe. White was elected to serve as chairman of the commission, and Morgan was elected vice-chairman. In addition to the appointed members, Paul A. Johnston, director of the Department of Administration, was elected to serve as executive secretary. When Mr. Johnston resigned, State Property Officer Frank B. Turner was selected to replace him.

The commission selected Edward Durell Stone of New York and John S. Holloway and Ralph B. Reeves Jr. of Raleigh to serve as architectural consultants. After a thorough study by the commission, the site selected for construction was a 5½-acre area one block north of the Capitol. This site, encompassing two blocks, is bounded by Jones, Salisbury, Lane, and Wilmington Streets. A section of Halifax Street between Jones and Lane was closed and made a part of the new site. Bids on the new building were received in December 1960, and construction began in early 1961.

The 1961 General Assembly appropriated an additional one million dollars for furnishings and equipment, bringing the total appropriation to $5.5 million, or $1.24 for each citizen of North Carolina based on 1960 census figures.

The consulting architects wrote the following description of the new building:

> The State Legislative Building, though not an imitation of historic classical styles, is classical in character. Rising from a 340-foot wide podium of North Carolina granite, the building proper is 242 feet square. The walls and the columns are of Vermont marble, the latter forming a colonnade encompassing the building and reaching 24 feet from the podium to the roof of the second floor.
>
> Inset in the south podium floor, at the main entrance, is a 28-foot diameter terrazzo mosaic of the Great Seal of the State. From the first floor main entrance (on Jones Street) the carpeted 22-foot wide main stair extends directly to the third floor and the public galleries of the

Senate and House, the auditorium, the display area, and the roof gardens.

The four garden courts are located at the corners of the building. These courts contain tropical plants, and three have pools, fountains, and hanging planters. The main floor areas of the courts are located on the first floor, and galleries overlook the courts from the mezzanine floor. The skylights which provide natural lighting are located within the roof gardens overhead. The courts provide access to committee rooms in the first floor, the legislative chambers in the second floor, and to members' offices in both floors.

The Senate and House chambers, each 5,180 square feet in area, occupy the east and west wings of the second floor. Following the traditional relationship of the two chambers in the Capitol, the two spaces are divided by the rotunda; and when the main brass doors are open, the two presiding officers face one another. Each pair of brass doors weighs 1,500 pounds.

The five pyramidal roofs covering the Senate and House chambers, the auditorium, the main stair, and the rotunda are sheathed with copper, as is the Capitol. The pyramidal shape of the roofs are visible in the pointed ceilings inside. The structural ribs form a coffered ceiling; and inside the coffered patterns are concentric patterns outlined in gold. In each chamber, the distance from the floor to the peak of the ceiling is 45 feet.

Chandeliers in the chambers and the main stair are 8 feet in diameter and weigh 625 pounds each. The 12-foot diameter chandelier of the rotunda, like the others, is of brass, but its weight is 750 pounds.

Because of the interior climate, the garden courts and rotunda have tropical plants and trees. Outside, however, the shrubs and trees are of the indigenous type. Among the trees on the grounds and on the roof areas are sugar maples, dogwoods, crabapples, magnolias, crepe myrtles, and pines.

Throughout the building, the same color scheme is maintained: Walnut accented with white, gold and red, and green foliage. In general, all wood is American walnut, metal is brass or similar material, carpets are red, and upholstery is gold or black.

The enclosed area consists of 206,000 square feet of floor area with a volume of 3,210,000 cubic feet. Heating equipment provides over 7,000,000 B.T.U.s per hour; and the cooling equipment has a capacity of 620 tons. For lighting, motors, and other electrical equipment, the building has a connected service load of over 2,000,000 watts.

The main staircase in the Legislative Building.

Additional renovations have been completed to create more office space and improve on meeting room facilities needed for the various committees of the General Assembly. In 1982, the Legislative Office Building was opened and while the first occupants were the Department of the Secretary of State on the third floor and the state auditor on the second, the majority of the space currently is used by the legislature. Nearly half of the members of each house moved to new offices in the building as well as several of the support divisions of Legislative Services.

Outside, an underground water reclamation system was installed in 2005. It captures stormwater runoff from the building and condensation from air-conditioning units, then uses it for irrigation of the grounds.

THE EXECUTIVE RESIDENCES OF NORTH CAROLINA

North Carolina's first legislators were traveling men. With no "fixed seat of government," early members of the General Assembly traveled from plantation to plantation and town to town until 1792 when a capital (Raleigh) was planned and laid out in the "woods of Wake." The new city was named in honor of the Elizabethan patron of early colonization, Sir Walter Raleigh. Shortly thereafter, the legislature enacted a law requiring the governor to reside at the permanent seat of government. Samuel Ashe of New Hanover County, elected in 1795, was the first governor to be affected by this law. He expressed his reaction emphatically: ". . . it was never supposed that a Man annually elected to the Chief Magistracy would commit such folly as to attempt the building of a House at the seat of Government in which he might for a time reside." The committee of the General Assembly to which Ashe's letter was referred hastened to inform him that the law was enacted before he was elected and could be considered "as a condition under the incumbrance of which he accepted the appointment."

Despite its pointed pronouncement, the General Assembly took steps to provide a dwelling for chief executives, instructing the state treasurer to purchase or lease a suitable house. In 1797, a plain two-story frame building painted white and an office for the governor were provided on Lot 131, the southwest corner of Fayetteville and Hargett Streets. The house proved hopelessly inadequate by 1810, as stated in a letter from Gov. Benjamin Smith:

> But we shall have time to retrace our steps for the House allotted by the State for the Chief Magistrate is in such order that it is agreed by all who view it, not to be fit for the family of a decent tradesman, and certainly none could be satisfied; even if safe in it, but this is questionable. The late storm has thrown off a considerable part of one of the chimneys and cracked some of the remainder. The plaster is frequently falling, and the roof is so leaky that in going from the sitting rooms to the chambers during a rain a wetting is experienced.

To remedy this situation, the General Assembly of 1813 appointed a committee to provide better facilities, and plans were drawn for the erection of a more suitable dwelling. The members selected a site at the foot of Fayetteville Street facing the old State House. Money from the sale of public lands was to pay construction costs. In 1816, an elaborate brick structure with white-columned porticoes was completed, and Gov. William Miller became the first occupant of the "Governor's Palace."

Twenty succeeding governors resided in the "Palace," as it was cynically termed, and much of the history of the state centered there.

French soldier and statesman, the Marquis de Lafayette, was an overnight guest in 1825. Some sessions of the General Assembly were held in the building following the burning of the State House in 1831. Zebulon Baird Vance (1862-1864; 1864-1865; 1877-1879) was the last governor to occupy the Palace.

Union general William T. Sherman and his staff were quartered in the Palace during the spring of 1865. Although as unwelcome guests they may have injured the pride of local citizens, occupying forces caused only minor damage to the house. Years of neglect, however, made the Palace unattractive to governors and their families. During the Reconstruction period, until the completion of the present Mansion in 1891, successive chief executives resided in Raleigh, living in rented houses, hotel rooms, or—during two administrations—in their own homes. From 1871 to 1891, a noted Raleigh hotel, the Yarborough House, served as the unofficial residence for several governors.

In 1879, the last year of Governor Vance's third term, a commission appointed two years earlier by the General Assembly to investigate the possibilities of providing a suitable residence for North Carolina's governors issued a report of its findings. The commission had been charged with the task of selling unused state lands in, and adjacent to, the city of Raleigh, including the Governor's Palace and its grounds. Proceeds from the sales were earmarked for the construction of a house and outbuildings suitable for the governor.

Opinions varied concerning the proposed project. In the matter of location, several members thought it advantageous to build a new dwelling on a lot adjacent to the Capitol, but were convinced the commission did not have the authority to do so. Others favored building an executive mansion on Burke Square, while the majority wanted to renovate the old Palace. Despite spirited debates, the commission did agree that even without a special appropriation, a new house could be built through the sale of the Palace and other state property. Because of the general lack of consensus, however, the commission merely reported its accomplishments and awaited further legislative orders.

The decision to build the present Executive Mansion was finally approved by the General Assembly through the efforts and perseverance

The Executive Mansion in Raleigh, North Carolina. Photograph courtesy of the Executive Mansion Fine Arts Committee.

of Gov. Thomas J. Jarvis (1879-1885). A bill ratified in February 1883 authorized the construction of a house on Burke Square, provided some furnishings, and required the governor to occupy it upon completion. The governor and the council of state were directed to use convict labor and such materials as were "manufactured or prepared, either in whole or in part" at the penitentiary, when such a procedure seemed feasible. Governor Jarvis reasoned that given the construction work then being done at the state penitentiary, a savings could be realized by purchasing larger quantities of building materials and employing convict labor in the construction of the Mansion simultaneously. Furthermore, from a practical standpoint, Jarvis thought the state would profit by having both of the projects under the same management. Experienced businessmen advised that such a plan might save the state as much as $20,000.

The penitentiary board, recognizing the law required it to furnish the major portion of labor and materials for the Executive Mansion, authorized the warden and architect of the penitentiary, William J. Hicks, "to enter into a contract according to the specifications laid before us for the building of the house for the sum of twenty-five thousand dollars." The council of state accepted this arrangement. Two months after passage of the bill, the council of state met with the governor to discuss financing the project. The governor was to use money from an earlier (1877) sale of state lands, to sell the old Palace and grounds, and to employ an architect to draft sketches and specifications for the council's consideration. Expenditures were not to exceed the funds available, and money to be spent by the governor and council was to be placed in an itemized account under the strict supervision of the auditor.

Nominees for an architect were then considered. The superintendent of construction for the State Capitol, David Paton, was suggested, but because of the architect's advanced age, he was unable to take on the assignment. The council selected Samuel Sloan of Philadelphia and his assistant, Adolphus Gustavus Bauer, and received Sloan's designs from him personally when he arrived in Raleigh on April 26, 1883. A Raleigh *News and Observer* reporter declared the designs "very artistic, representing an ornate building, in modern style, three stories in height, with the ample porches, hall ways, and windows which every house built in this climate should have." On May 7, the Sloan designs were accepted with minor modifications suggested by some of Raleigh's "able builders."

During the early stages of construction, a report issued by the officers of the penitentiary board in mid-1884 declared the building "handsome in design, constructed of the best material by the best workers." Masons used pressed brick made at the prison for the construction of the Mansion and later for the walks surrounding it. The exterior of the Mansion was trimmed with North Carolina sandstone. Prison officials expressed satisfaction with the artistry and convenience of the interior of the house and wished to enhance it further by using "an elaborate North Carolina hard-wood finish." A progress report issued by Governor Jarvis in 1885 noted that stone for the residence was quarried in Anson County, and, even though the building fund was nearly depleted, the governor strongly argued for the original plan to use native, North Carolina hardwoods in the ceiling, wainscoting, and woodwork. It would, he said, "attract attention to our wealth of timber," be "beautiful and cheap," and a "source of pride to every citizen in the state." The legislature was not swayed, however, and approved no new funds during that session.

After Gov. Alfred M. Scales's swearing in on January 21, 1885, construction slowed dramatically, and, in April 1887, stopped completely. The Mansion was closed up and by year's end was being derisively referred to as "Jarvis's Folly." Certainly, commitment to completing the project was neither widespread nor steadfast, partly because of the opposition from legislators who represented a largely rural population. Tough economic times prompted questions about the wisdom and fairness of appropriating funds for the grand house. In fact, in March 1889, the state senate passed a bill authorizing the sale of the Mansion, but the house rejected it. Eventually, however, using funds raised mostly through the sale of state property (i.e., the Pettigrew Hospital, parts of the old Palace grounds, and city lots owned by the state), William Hicks would manage to complete the project, insufficient though the resources were for meeting the original building specifications. The results of cost cutting and the Mansion's brief abandonment were eventually apparent.

In November 1889, before the Mansion was occupied, repair and preservation work had already begun with "certain exterior and interior painting" of the woodwork. Most of the accounts emphasize the deplorable condition of the completed house, including cheap plumbing and the use of dirt as soundproofing beneath floors. The third floor and the basement had been left unfinished. On the Mansion grounds were horse stables and other dependencies. Drinking water was pumped by a small gasoline engine from two cisterns in the basement to a tank located on the third floor.

By December 1890, the Mansion was nearly finished, but Gov. Daniel Fowle (1889-1891) did not move in until January 5, 1891. He was particularly anxious to occupy the house in view of earlier attempts to abandon it as a residence for the governor. Although the earliest laws providing for construction of the residence had allowed for the purchase of furnishings, mounting construction costs meant only a small portion of the funds set aside for this remained. Former governor and Mrs. Jarvis had made some purchases as early as 1883, and Governor Scales reported in 1887 that he had obtained some furniture from the old Palace. Even so, Fowle brought his own furniture to make up the deficit in the Mansion, setting a precedent followed for many years until the house was adequately furnished. To avoid confusion over ownership of the Mansion furnishings, he methodically filed a list of his personal belongings with the state treasurer. In 1891, additional furniture purchases were made with an appropriation of $1,500. Only three months after he moved into the Mansion, Governor Fowle's term of office was cut short by his sudden death on April 7, 1891. His term was filled by Lt. Gov. Thomas Holt.

Holt's successor, Elias Carr, was the first governor to live in the Mansion for a full four-year term (1893-1897). Like his predecessors, he found the house in need of furnishings and repairs. Funds were allocated by the legislature in February 1893 for furniture, maintenance, and minor improvements. Two years later, another appropriation made landscaping the grounds possible. Brick walkways and driveway entrance posts were installed in 1896.

Shortly after the inauguration of Gov. Daniel Russell (1897-1901), the General Assembly appointed a committee to examine the Mansion and recommend needed alterations. The committee found that several repairs were needed and promptly introduced a resolution to provide the necessary money. In March 1897, an appropriation of $600 was allotted for the Mansion's upkeep. Near the end of Russell's administration, George Washington Vanderbilt donated evergreen trees for the grounds.

As the nineteenth century closed, a permanent residence for the state's chief executives more commodious than its predecessors was at last established in the capital, one that reflected the progressive vitality and spirit of North Carolina and its people. Similarly, during the early 1900s, North Carolina's governors moved the state forward with progressive new programs designed to benefit a society that was predominantly agricultural. Of primary importance was upgrading the educational system and establishing industries that would bring new jobs and additional revenues to the state. The administrations of Governors Aycock, Glenn, Kitchin, and Craig emphasized these aims. During their terms, the Executive Mansion continued to serve as the center of Tar Heel hospitality. If a 1909 Raleigh guidebook description is any indication, "Jarvis's Folly" had not been so fanciful after all. It deemed the structure "one of the most beautiful and picturesque buildings in the city," and moreover, noted that, "every North Carolinian has a feeling of pride in his State as he gazes on the home provided for his Governor." It had, as Jarvis predicted, come to be a treasure of which our state could be proud.

As the years passed, however, the need for major repairs to the residence became more evident. Like other incoming governors, Thomas Bickett (1917-1921) began his term with an inspection of the Mansion and recommendations for its improvement. The superintendent of buildings and grounds made a detailed report, and Mrs. Bickett submitted suggestions for interior renovations by architect James A. Salter, along with his cost estimates. Her plea resulted in the introduction of a bill that requested $65,000 for repairs and renovations. This optimistic bill failed to pass the General Assembly, and a substitute measure was enacted in March 1917 allowing a paltry $4,000 "to renovate, equip, and properly furnish the Governor's Mansion and improve the surrounding grounds." Later that same year, the legislature approved an additional $4,000 for furnishings, and in 1919, appropriated $4,000 more for continued refurbishment. During

The entrance hallway. Photograph by Leslie Wright Dow, courtesy of the Executive Mansion Fine Arts Committee.

the 1920 renovations, the second floor ballroom, which had been used to billet overnight groups of as many as sixty soldiers during World War I, was divided by walls to form bedrooms, baths, closets, and a private corridor to connect several of the family bedrooms. Mrs. Bickett purchased dining room furniture and a four-poster bed for the guestroom at the top of the Grand Staircase—the room where President Harry S. Truman was to sleep in 1948.

As preparations were made for Gov. Angus W. McLean's residence in the Mansion (1925-1929), the previous renovations were deemed inadequate. Secretary of State W. N. Everett made his own examination and reported that major repairs could provide the governor with a comfortable dwelling. Everett suggested a sum of $50,000 for repairs and new furnishings. Although this action was taken without McLean's knowledge, upon learning of it, he became active in seeking the appropriation. Thus, Everett and Governor McLean must be credited not only with saving the Mansion, but also with making it, for the first time, a house in keeping with the dignity of the governor and his office.

Concurrent with Everett's work, and shortly after his inauguration, McLean requested that the State Board of Health, required to inspect all state institutions for sanitation, examine the Mansion, which it did in February 1925. The inspection report was startling. Rated on the same basis as hotels, the Mansion received "the very low rating of 71." The report added that the management of a hotel receiving such a rating would be subject to indictment. The principal deductions in scoring were for uncleanliness.

Dust pervaded the atmosphere, covering the woodwork, filming the furniture, and stifling the air. Indeed, Governor Fowle's contemporaries had described clouds of dust following in the walker's footsteps. From his time until the revealing inspection, little had been done to alleviate the condition. The basement, extending beneath the entire house, had a dirt floor with the exception of two small rooms floored with decaying wood. This deficiency allowed dirt to filter up through the unclosed registers of an earlier heating system. The hot water heater room and its entrance were paved with worn, irregular bricks, which, without proper drainage, weakened the foundations of the Mansion.

The first floor walls and floors were unsound, and the ornate plasterwork was disintegrating in some areas. From the small, poorly equipped, and inadequately ventilated kitchen area, cooking odors and greasy smoke were released into adjoining rooms, causing frequent embarrassment to the state's first family.

The upstairs floors, with boards five and six inches in width, of uneven and poor material, had half-inch cracks between them. Plumbers and steamfitters had removed these boards during earlier repairs, not bothering to nail them back down. They would spring and creak when walked upon and were practically impossible to keep clean. In the governor's room, the carpet was nearly worn through because of the uneven surface of the floor. The bathrooms, with linoleum flooring, papered walls, antique plumbing, and inaccessible corners were equally impossible to clean. The third or attic floor remained unfinished. Dust from large piles of rubbish and lime mortar sifted through ceiling light fixtures and wire openings into the bedrooms and baths below.

Consultants suggested obvious remedies: putting in a concrete floor, drains, and a ceiling in the basement; painting the ceilings and walls of the kitchen and butler's pantry; enlarging the kitchen with new floors and proper equipment, including a ventilator and smoke hood for the stove; refinishing floors and laying new floors; closing old heat registers and openings in the walls; tiling and wainscoting bathrooms and installing modern plumbing and electrical fixtures; properly sealing lighting fixture openings in ceilings; and covering floors with an inexpensive, but serviceable material.

Once money became available, the architectural firm of Atwood and Nash was employed to carry out the renovations. H. Pier-Giavina, a decorative artist from Wilmington, North Carolina, aided with the interior decoration. He recommended ivory, or some other light color, for the first floor woodwork and ordered round rosettes to cover openings in the walls. Workers removed as many as seven layers of wallpaper in order to carry out the new decorating scheme. Contractors also enclosed the plumbing and electrical wiring of the kitchen within the walls, thereby increasing safety.

Elizabeth Thompson, a local interior decorator and antique dealer, helped direct the refurbishment, with additional suggestions by Mrs. McLean. Workers bundled up and shipped off worn rugs to be rewoven and old furniture to be reupholstered. New carpets and draperies were purchased out of the annual appropriation for the upkeep of the Mansion. Governor McLean found money to finish a part of the third floor as servants' quarters. In addition, workers installed a cloakroom for women on the first floor and added a gentlemen's cloakroom, a servant's room, and offices for the governor in the basement.

The renovations greatly increased the value of the Mansion. In July 1926, Governor McLean informed Insurance Commissioner Stacy Wade that the $80,000 evaluation of the house was inadequate and that the Mansion could not be replaced for less than $200,000. The house had been constructed of the finest materials, and the interior, within the past year, had been completely renovated. A newspaper account, lauding Governor McLean's accomplishments, claimed that renovating a building considered by some as eligible for demolition had saved the state more than a third of a million dollars.

The renovation undertaken by Governor McLean was not fully completed during his term of office. Governor-elect O. Max Gardner (1929-1933) asked the Board of Public Buildings and Grounds to confer with the McLeans to determine the Mansion's remaining needs, and the General Assembly established a "Special Furniture and Equipment Account Available for [the] Incoming Governor." At the beginning of the Gardner administration, the General Assembly authorized the State Highway Commission to build and maintain walkways and drives "within the Mansion Square." Included in this project was a plan for the landscaping of the Mansion grounds. The state contracted with a prominent Philadelphia landscape architect, Thomas W. Sears, for the work. At Mrs. Gardner's suggestion, the exterior woodwork of the house was painted brown to blend with the sandstone and brickwork.

Later administrations brought further improvements and added comforts in order to keep pace with the times. An elevator was installed, air conditioning units were placed in some rooms, and a bomb shelter was added during Gov. Luther H. Hodges's term (1954-1961). Mrs. Terry Sanford added many antique furnishings during her husband's term of office (1961-1965). While the legislature endeavored to make the Mansion functional and livable, funds for major projects were inadequate. Therefore, in early 1965, Mrs. Dan K. Moore appointed an Executive Mansion Fine Arts Advisory Committee (EMFAC). In August, she announced that Mrs. Lorraine Pearce of Washington, D.C., the first curator of the White House, had been employed

The Rose Room. Photograph by Rick Alexander and Tim Buchman, courtesy of the Executive Mansion Fine Arts Committee.

as a consultant to the committee. In November 1965, Mrs. Pearce conducted the committee on a detailed tour of the Mansion and made specific suggestions for each room. Following a suggestion by Mrs. Pearce, Mrs. Moore and the EMFAC sponsored a tea in June 1966 to solicit funds for Mansion furnishings. Guests received brochures listing fine antique and reproduction furniture, rugs, and accessories suggested for purchase through donations. In 1967, the General Assembly officially created the Executive Mansion Fine Arts Commission, thus perpetuating the program of the first committee. Six years later, the General Assembly returned the commission to its original committee status.

A previously neglected area of the Mansion was the central hallway at the head of the Grand Staircase. Mrs. Moore conceived the idea of furnishing the area with representative pieces in recognition of North Carolina as the "furniture capital of the world." She contacted manufacturers who, in turn, requested the American Institute of Interior Designers to plan the area. Industries contributed furniture, accessories, and services to reappoint the hallway as an attractive and comfortable living area for the governor and his family. Another special project was the acquisition of a collection of North Carolina books for the Mansion library. Volumes by Tar Heel authors, as well as books about the state and her citizens, were acquired in the late 1960s.

A legislative appropriation of $58,000 financed renovation of the institutional kitchen facilities, providing a new freezer, expansion of the food preparation area into the basement, and a dumbwaiter-conveyor belt system to move trays from the first floor. Extending the garage area, landscaping, and lighting the grounds contributed to the efficiency and beauty of the Mansion. For added security, a decorative brick and wrought iron wall was constructed around the perimeter of Burke Square in early 1969.

Gov. Robert W. Scott (1969-1973) appreciated the historical significance of the building but felt it was time to review the Mansion's practical uses. The governor pointed out the old cast-iron radiators controlled by a single thermostat, the overloaded electrical circuits, the lack of a fire escape, and other hazards that needed correction. The front entrance hall chandelier, which had fallen in 1969 (fortunately without injuring anyone), aptly illustrated his concerns. Because of inadequate living conditions in the Mansion, the 1971 General Assembly established a seven-member Executive Residence Building Commission to develop and submit plans for a new official residence for the chief executive. The governor appointed an advisory committee that included former first ladies, state agency heads, and the mayor of Raleigh to work with the commission. Members of the commission inspected nine executive residences in other states and received

The South Porch. Photograph by Rick Alexander and Tim Buchman, courtesy of the Executive Mansion Fine Arts Committee.

presentations from six architectural firms being considered for the project. Upon review of the proposed designs for a new Executive Mansion (which, incidentally, were not well received), the legislature was informed that it would be more feasible to renovate the Burke Square residence than to construct a modern dwelling.

In May 1973, the General Assembly ratified "An Act to Appropriate Funds to Renovate the Governor's Mansion and to Make It Suitable as Both a Public Residence and a Private Residence for the Governor." The act specified:

> Removal of the existing heating system and installation of a year-round air conditioning system.
> Rewiring of the structure as needed to provide safe, adequate and convenient electrical circuits throughout the structure.
> Installation of a family kitchen on the second floor level.
> Installation of a fire escape from the third floor at the rear of the Mansion.
> Renovation and modernization of all bathrooms.
> Weatherstripping, repair, and reconstruction as necessary of all windows and frames in the building.
> Restoration of exterior brick walls.

This renovation was the most extensive in the history of the Executive Mansion. The General Assemblies of 1973 and 1975 appropriated funds amounting to $845,000. Gov. James E. Holshouser Jr. and his family relinquished use of the Mansion and moved into a temporary home in the Foxcroft suburb of Raleigh for eight months while interior renovations were carried out by F. Carter Williams, a local architectural firm. Because of the size and complexity of the project, Marie Sharpe Ham, the state interior design consultant, and the staff of the Division, now Office, of Archives and History assisted.

As work proceeded, it was discovered that most of the deterioration had been caused by water seepage within the walls. Portions of the decorative plaster ceilings had to be reconstructed and exterior and interior woodwork repaired or replaced with materials removed from elsewhere in the Mansion. The Grand Staircase was found to be constructed of rare North Carolina heart pine. Research showed the wood had originally been varnished and stained. An unpainted pine mantel on the third floor served as a guide for refinishing the staircase. Original carved paneling beneath windows and above doorways was discovered behind false panels, which were removed in order to reveal these unique design features.

In an effort to save money and promote state industry, materials produced within North Carolina were used in the renovation. Brick for the stair tower was selected to match that of the exterior. The state's textile industry assisted in replacing carpets and draperies. In addition, individuals and businesses donated decorative pieces for the enrichment of the furnishings collection (managed by the Department of Cultural Resources). Mrs. Holshouser later stated, "Our determination to emphasize North Carolina products clearly carries through the theme that Governor Jarvis had when he first envisioned a new Executive Mansion."

This determination carried over to the administration of Gov. James B. Hunt Jr. (1977-1985), the first governor of this state to be twice elected to successive four-year terms. The Mansion served as an adjunct to his Capitol office and as a regular meeting place for his cabinet and staff. Changes to the Mansion during his tenure included planting a vegetable garden, installing a chair lift for handicapped visitors, enclosing the east back porch in glass to serve as a morning room, refurbishing some first- and second-floor rooms, and outfitting the third floor with a recreation room—a retreat for the sports-minded Hunt family. Other events of note were the 1981 publication of a book on North Carolina's first ladies sponsored by former first lady Jeanelle Moore, and the establishment in 1983 of the Bailey-Tucker House on East Lane Street as the state's official guesthouse.

Gov. James G. Martin (1985-1993) became the second chief executive to serve successive terms. As the Mansion entered its second century of service to North Carolina's governors, a Victorian garden, a shade and play garden, and rose and herb gardens were planted on the grounds of the Mansion; all were financed by private contributions. Unfinished third-floor space was converted into an office for the first lady in 1989. A major interior refurbishment was carried out to commemorate the building's centennial in 1991 and for the viewing pleasure of more than 50,000 annual visitors. The Executive Mansion Fund, Inc., a nonprofit 501(c)3 organization, raised over two million dollars for preserving and maintaining the house and its furnishings. This fund also supports educational publications and programs.

THE GOVERNOR'S WESTERN RESIDENCE

Originally built in the mid-1940s as a vacation house for a private citizen, this three-bedroom, six thousand square foot home is located approximately three miles from Asheville, overlooking Beaver Lake. The Asheville Chamber of Commerce later purchased it using private donations. During Gov. Terry Sanford's administration (1961-1965), the city of Asheville donated the house to the state for use by the governor. Now known as the "Governor's Western Residence," it is used by governors and their families as a retreat, by government officials on state business, and by civic groups for meetings and receptions.

Photograph by Charles Jones, courtesy of the Executive Mansion Fine Arts Committee.

Additionally, a grass-roots organization, Friends of the Executive Mansion, contributes to renovation and preservation work. Concurrently, in the North Carolina mountains, the Governor's Western Residence received its own improvements. The kitchen was fully renovated, the entire house refurbished, and fund-raising and plans for a large picnic pavilion completed. A documentary video about the Mansion and a hardback book detailing the Mansion's first one hundred years were also produced during the Martin administration.

From 1993 to 2001, Gov. James Hunt Jr. returned to the Mansion, and, as during his previous terms, used it as a supplemental office. The need for a full renovation of the Executive Mansion was recognized, and all plans and funding were arranged. In the meantime, the Western Residence picnic pavilion was constructed, all patio windows replaced, a new heating and air system installed, and a conference room remodeled. A book entitled, *The First Ladies of North Carolina*, last revised in 1987, was totally rewritten and updated in 2000 as *North Carolina's First Ladies, 1891-2001, Who Have Resided in the Executive Mansion at 200 North Blount Street.*

To an even greater extent than his predecessor, Gov. Michael F. Easley (2001–present) has used the Executive Mansion for work, meetings, bill signings, entertaining, and presentations. Although an extensive new security system was donated and installed in 2003-2004 and a refurbishment of the second floor undertaken, other work planned during Governor Hunt's third and fourth terms was suspended because of a budget crisis. Some work could not be avoided, however. The state had spent one million dollars to clean mold before the Easleys moved in. In 2005, the dangerous mold was back, and the Secretary of Administration declared a state of emergency. The Easleys vacated the mansion for nearly six months while workers cleaned, waterproofed, replaced insulation, and installed a new ventilation system. The extensive but necessary repairs totaled over four million dollars. The architect in charge said it was the worst case of mold infestation he had ever seen.

North Carolina is proud to have one of the few governors' residences in the nation constructed in the nineteenth century that is still in use. Architecturally, it is a fine example of the Queen Anne cottage style popular during the American Victorian period, while the exterior wooden ornamentation is typical of the decorative Eastlake style, so named for the English architect, Charles Eastlake. The Executive Mansion stands today rooted in the past, but well appointed and equipped to meet the expanding needs and challenges of the future. For over one hundred years, the time, talent, funds, and devotion of North Carolinians have contributed to the continuing tradition of gracious hospitality to all who enter its doors.

THE GREAT SEAL OF THE STATE OF NORTH CAROLINA

A seal for important documents was used before a state government was ever implemented in North Carolina. During the colonial period, North Carolina used, successively, four different seals. Since independence, six seals have been used.

Shortly after King Charles II issued the Charter of 1663 to the Lords Proprietors, a seal was adopted to use in conjunction with their newly acquired domains in America. No official description has been found of the seal, but it can be seen in the British Public Record Office in London. The seal has two sides and is 3 3/8 inches in diameter. The impression was made by bonding two wax cakes together with tape before being impressed. The finished impression was about one-fourth of an inch thick. This seal was used on all official papers of the Lords Proprietors of Carolina.

front *back*

Seal of the Lords Proprietors of Carolina

When the government of Albemarle County was organized in 1665, it adopted for a seal the reverse side of the seal of the Lords Proprietors. Between the coats of arms, the word A-L-BE-M-A-R-L-E was fixed in capitals, beginning with the letter *A* between the Craven arms and those of Lord John Berkeley.

Seal of the Government of Albemarle and Province of North Carolina, 1665–1729

The Albemarle seal was small, only 1 7/16 inches in diameter, and had only one face. The seal was usually impressed on red wax, but was occasionally seen imprinted on a wafer stuck to the instrument with soft wax. The government for Albemarle County was the first to use the seal; however, as the colony grew, it became the seal of the entire Province of North Carolina. It continued in use until just after the purchase of North Carolina by the Crown. During the troublesome times of the Cary Rebellion,* the Albemarle seal was not used. Instead, Thomas Cary used his family arms as a seal for official papers. William Glover used his private seal during his presidency as well.

When North Carolina became a royal colony in 1729, the old "Albemarle" seal was no longer applicable. On February 3, 1730, the Board of Trade recommended that the king order a public seal for the Province of North Carolina. Later that same month, the king approved the recommendations and ordered that a new seal be prepared for the governor of North Carolina. On March 25, the Board of Trade presented the king with a draft of the proposed seal for his consideration. The king approved the proposal on April 10 with one

---

* The Lords Proprietors commissioned Edward Hyde as governor in 1710 to replace Thomas Cary. Cary challenged Hyde's authority, and armed conflict erupted between the two men and their supporters. The fighting ended with Cary's arrest on charges of sedition and rebellion. He was sent to England for trial but released for lack of evidence. Hyde continued as governor until his death on September 8, 1712.

front   *back*

Seal of the Province of North Carolina, 1730-1767

minor change. The chief engraver of seals, Rollos, was ordered to "engrave a silver Seal according to said draught."

The arrival of the new seal was delayed, so when the council met in Edenton on March 30, 1731, the old seal of the colony was ordered to be used until the new one arrived. The new seal reached the colony in late April, and the messenger delivering it from Cape Fear was paid ten pounds for his journey. The impression of the new seal was made by placing two cakes or layers of wax together, and then interlacing ribbon or tape with the attached seal between the wax cakes. It was customary to put a piece of paper on the outside of the cakes before they were impressed. The complete seal was 4 3/8 inches in diameter and from one-half to five-eights inches thick and weighed about 5 ½ ounces.

At a meeting of the council in New Bern on December 14, 1767, Governor Tryon produced a new Great Seal of the province with His Majesty's Royal Warrant bearing date at the Court of St. James the 9th day of July 1767. The old seal was returned to His Majesty's Council office at Whitehall. Accompanying the warrant was a description of the new seal with instructions that it was to be used in sealing all patents and grants of land, and all public instruments passed in the king's name for service within the province. It was four inches in diameter, one-half to five-eighths inches thick, and weighed 4½ ounces.

Sometimes a smaller seal than the Great Seal was used on commissions and grants, such as a small heart-shaped seal or one in the

Seal of the Province of North Carolina, 1767-1776

shape of an ellipse. These impressions were evidently made by putting the wax far enough under the edge of the Great Seal to take the impression of the crown. The royal governors also used their private seals on commissions and grants.

Lord Granville, after the sale of the colony by the Lords Proprietors, retained his right to issue land grants. He used his private seal on the grants he issued. The last reference found to the colonial seal is in a letter from Gov. Josiah Martin to the Earl of Hillsborough in November 1771, in which he recounts the broken condition of the seal. He states the seal had been repaired and though "awkwardly mended . . . [it was] in such manner as to answer all purposes."

Following independence, Section XVII of the new constitution adopted at Halifax on December 18, 1776, provided "That there shall be a Seal of this State, which shall be kept by the Governor, and used by him as occasion may require; and shall be called the Great Seal of the State of North Carolina, and be affixed to all grants and commissions." When a new constitution was adopted in 1868, Article III, Section 16 provided for "a seal of the State, which shall be kept by the Governor, and used by him, as occasion may require, and shall be called The Great Seal of the State of North Carolina." It also provided for the secretary of state to countersign all grants and commissions with the governor. When the people of North Carolina ratified the current constitution in

1970, Article III, Section 10 contained provisions for "The Great Seal of the State of North Carolina." However, the wording that authorized the secretary of state to countersign documents was removed.

On December 22, 1776, the Provincial Congress at Halifax appointed William Hooper, Joseph Hewes, and Thomas Burke as commissioners to procure a seal for the state; however, there is no record that a report was ever made by this commission. The Congress provided for the governor to use his "private seal at arms" until the Great Seal for the state was procured. A bill calling for the procurement of a Great Seal was introduced in the lower house of the General Assembly on April 28, 1778. The bill became law on May 2. The legislation provided that William Tisdale, Esq., be appointed to cut and engrave a seal for the state. On November 7, 1779, the senate granted Tisdale £150 to make the seal. The seal procured under this act was used until 1794. The actual size of the seal was three inches in diameter and one-fourth inch thick. It was made by putting two cakes of wax together with paper wafers on the outside and pressing them between the dies, thus forming the front and back of the seal. An official

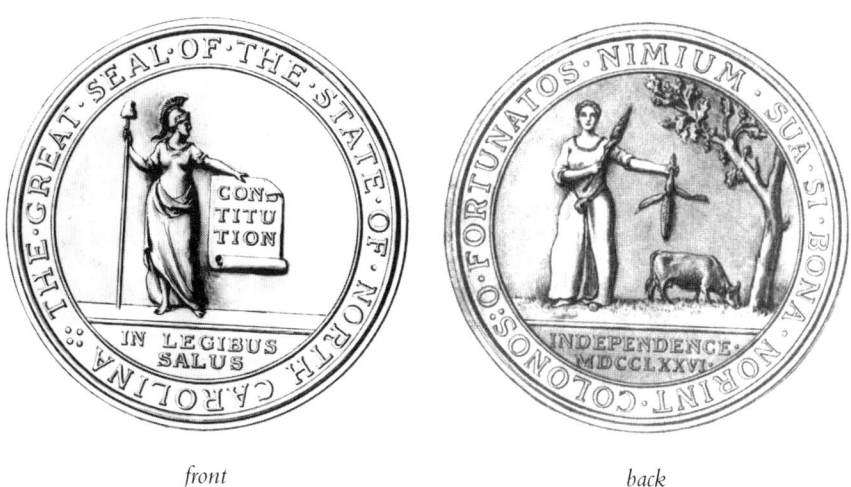

front　　　　　　　　　　　　　　*back*

The Great Seal of the State of North Carolina, 1779-1794

description of this seal has not been found, but many of the ones still in existence are in an almost perfect state of preservation.

In January 1792, the General Assembly authorized a new state seal, requiring that it be prepared with only one side. Col. Abisha Thomas, an agent of North Carolina commissioned by Gov. Alexander Martin, was in Philadelphia to settle the state's Revolutionary War claims against the federal government. Martin sent a design to Colonel Thomas for a new seal for the state; however, after suggestions by Dr. Hugh Williamson and Sen. Samuel Johnston, this sketch was discarded and a new one submitted. This new sketch, with some modification, was finally accepted by Gov. Richard Dobbs Spaight, and Colonel Thomas had the seal made accordingly.

The press for the old seal must have been very large and unwieldy, probably because of its two-sided nature and large diameter. Governor Spaight, in a letter to Colonel Thomas in February 1793, wrote: "Let the screws by which the impression is to be made be as portable as possible so as it may be adapted to our present itinerant government. The one now in use by which the Great Seal is at present made is so large and unwieldy as to be carried only in a cart or wagon and of course has become stationary at the Secretary's office which makes it very convenient." The seal was cut some time during the summer of 1793, and Colonel Thomas brought it home with him in time for the meeting of the legislature in November, at which session it was

The Great Seal of the State of North Carolina, 1794-1835

"approbated." The screw to the seal was 2½ in diameter and was used until around 1835.

In the winter of 1834-1835, the legislature enacted legislation authorizing the governor to procure a new seal. The preamble to the act stated that the old seal had been used since the first day of March 1793. A new seal, which was very similar to its predecessor, was adopted in 1835 and continued in use until 1893. In 1868, the legislature authorized the governor to procure a replacement seal and required him to do so whenever the old one was lost or so worn or defaced that it was unfit for use.

The Great Seal of the State of North Carolina, 1836-1893

In 1883, Col. Samuel McDowell Tate introduced a bill that did not provide that a new seal be procured, but described in detail what the seal should be like. In 1893, Jacob Battle introduced a bill that added at the foot of the coat of arms of the state as part thereof the motto, *Esse Quam Videri*, and provided that the date "May 20, 1775," be inscribed at the top of the coat of arms.

The Great Seal of the State of North Carolina, 1893–1971

By the early twentieth century, the ship that appeared in the background of the early seals had disappeared. The North Carolina mountains were the only backdrop on the seal, where formerly both the mountains and the ship had been depicted.

The various changes to the official seal illustrate the great liberty taken throughout our history with its design. The 1971 General Assembly, in an effort to "provide a standard for the Great Seal of the State of North Carolina," passed the following act amending the General Statutes provision relative to the state seal:

> The Governor shall procure for the State a seal, which shall be called the great seal of the State of North Carolina, and shall be two and one-quarter inches in diameter, and its design shall be a representation of the figures of Liberty and Plenty, looking toward each other, but not more than half-fronting each other and otherwise disposed as follows: Liberty, the first figure, standing, her pole with cap on it in her left hand and a scroll with the word "Constitution" inscribed thereon in her right hand. Plenty, the second figure, sitting down, her right arm half extended towards Liberty, three heads of grain in her right hand, and in her left, the small end of her horn, the mouth of which is resting at her feet, and the contents of the horn rolling out.

The background on the seal shall contain a depiction of mountains running from left to right to the middle of the seal and an ocean running from right to left to the middle of the seal. A side view of a three-masted ship shall be located on the ocean and to the right of Plenty. The date "May 20, 1775" shall appear within the seal and across the top of the seal and the words "esse quam videri" shall appear at the bottom around the perimeter. The words "THE GREAT SEAL of the STATE of NORTH CAROLINA" shall appear around the perimeter. No other words, figures or other embellishments shall appear on the seal.

It shall be the duty of the Governor to file in the office of Secretary of State an impression of the great seal, certified to under his hand and attested by the Secretary of State, which impression so certified the Secretary of State shall carefully preserve among the records of his Office.

The Great Seal of the State of North Carolina, 1971-1984

The late Jullian R. Allsbrook, who served in the North Carolina Senate for many years, felt that the adoption date of the Halifax Resolves ought to be commemorated on the state seal as it was already on the state flag. This was to serve "as a constant reminder of the people of this state's commitment to liberty." Legislation adding the date "April 12, 1776" to the Great Seal of North Carolina was ratified May 2, 1983, with an effective date of January 1, 1984. Chapter 257 of the Session Laws of North Carolina included a provision that "This act shall not invalidate any Seal presently on display or heretofore used."

The Great Seal of the State of North Carolina, 1984–present

In addition to the alterations of the images on the seal, the device and technique for imprinting the physical seal itself have also changed. Once a cake of wax impressed on both sides by an unwieldy press, the seal is now embossed either directly on the paper or in gold foil by a smaller, more portable press. Sometimes a short ribbon extends from the bottom of the seal, fastened between the foil and the document on which the foil has been impressed.

THE STATE FLAG

Ancient writings, paintings, and carvings tell of the use of flags among early civilizations like the Egyptians, Assyrians, Persians, and Hebrews. In early medieval Europe, flags bore religious significance, but with the rise of feudalism, they came to represent the distinct and numerous classes. As feudalism died out and nation states arose, so too did the flags to represent them.

Today, flags come in various shapes, colors, and sizes, and are most commonly known as emblems of countries, states, institutions, or organizations. The world over, national flags possess a common significance. They stand as the symbols of strength and unity, representing the national spirit and patriotism of the people over whom they fly. Of its citizens, a given flag commands respect, inspires patriotism, and instills loyalty both in peace and war. In this country, we have a national flag that stands as the emblem of our strength and unity as a nation, a tangible representation of our national spirit and honor.

In addition to our national flag, each state in the Union has a "state flag" that is symbolic of its own individuality and domestic ideals. The state flag expresses some particular trait, or commemorates some historical event of the state's people. Most state flags consist of the coat of arms of that state upon a suitably colored field. It is said that the first state flag of North Carolina was built on this model, but legislative records show that a "state flag" was not established or recognized until 1861. The constitutional convention of 1861, which passed the ordinance of secession, adopted a state flag. On May 20, 1861, the day the secession resolution was adopted, Col. John D. Whitford, a member of the convention from Craven County, introduced an ordinance, which was referred to a select committee of seven. The ordinance stated that the flag of this state shall be a blue field with a white *V* thereon, and a star, encircling which shall be the words, "*Sirgit astrum*, May 20, 1775."

Colonel Whitford was made chairman of the committee to which this ordinance was referred. The committee secured the aid and advice of William Jarl Browne, an artist of Raleigh. Browne prepared and submitted a model to this committee, and this model was adopted by the convention of June 22, 1861. The Browne model was vastly different from the original design proposed by Colonel Whitford. The law as it appears in the ordinance passed by the convention follows.

AN ORDINANCE IN RELATION TO A STATE FLAG

Be it ordained by this Convention, and it is hereby ordained by the authority of the same, That the Flag of North Carolina shall consist of a red field with a white star in the centre, and with the inscription, above the star, in a semi-circular form, of "May 20th, 1775," and below the star, in a semi-circular form, of "May 20th, 1861." That there shall be two bars of equal width, and the length of the field shall be equal to the bar, the width of the field being equal to both bars: the first bar shall be blue, and the second shall be white: and the length of the flag shall be one-third more than its width. [Ratified the 22nd day of June, 1861.]

This state flag is said to have been issued to North Carolina regiments of state troops during the summer of 1861 and borne by them throughout the war. It was the only flag, except the national and Confederate colors, used by North Carolina troops during the Civil War.

The 1861 flag was used until 1885 when the legislature adopted a new model. A bill introduced by Gen. Johnstone Jones on February 5, 1885, passed its final reading one month later after little debate. The act follows.

AN ACT TO ESTABLISH A STATE FLAG

The General Assembly of North Carolina do enact:

SECTION 1. That the flag of North Carolina shall consist of a blue union, containing in the centre thereof a white star with the letter N. in gilt on the left and the letter C. in gilt on the right of said star, the circle containing the same to be one-third the width of said union.

SEC. 2. That the fly of the flag shall consist of two equally proportioned bars; the upper bar to be red, the lower bar to be white; that the length of the bars horizontally shall be equal to the perpendicular length of the union, and the total length of the flag shall be one-third more than its width.

SEC. 3. That above the star in the centre of the union there shall be a gilt scroll in semi-circular form, containing in black letters this inscription: "May 20th, 1775," and that below the star there shall be a similar scroll containing in black letters the inscription: "April 12th, 1776."

SEC. 4. That this act shall take effect from and after its ratification.

In the General Assembly read three times, and ratified this 9th day of March, A.D. 1885.

It is interesting to examine the significance of the dates found on the flag. The first, "May 20th, 1775," refers to the so-called "Mecklenburg Declaration of Independence," a document that has been a source of controversy (see sidebar on pages 54 and 55). The second, appearing on the state flag of 1861, is "May 20th, 1861." This date commemorated

From the *North Carolina Manual, 1989-1990.*

the secession of the state from the Union, but as the cause for secession was defeated, this date no longer represented anything after the Civil War. So when a new flag was adopted in 1885, "May 20th, 1861" was replaced with "April 12th, 1776." This date commemorates the Halifax Resolves (also known as the Halifax Resolution), a document that places the Old North State in the very front rank, both in point of time and in spirit, among the colonies at the Constitutional Convention in Philadelphia that demanded unconditional freedom and absolute independence from any foreign power. Specifically, the Resolves officially and explicitly declared independence from the British Empire. This document stands out as one of the great landmarks in North Carolina history.

Since 1885, there have been no major changes in our state flag. However, in 1991, the General Assembly did approve minor modifications to the state flag. The commas in the dates were removed, and the total length of the flag was changed from being one-third more than its width to being one-half more than its width.

For some time after its adoption, the flag remained unknown and a stranger to the good people of our state. However, as time passed and we became more public spirited, the emblem of the Old North State assumed a station of greater prominence among our people. One sign of this increased interest was the act passed by the legislature of 1907, requiring the state flag to be flown above all state institutions, public buildings, and courthouses. In addition to this, many public and private schools, fraternal orders, and other organizations now fly the state flag. The people of the state should become acquainted with the emblem of that government to which they owe allegiance and from which they secure protection, and to ensure that they would, the legislature enacted the following act.

AN ACT TO PROMOTE GREATER LOYALTY AND RESPECT FOR THE SOVEREIGNTY OF THE STATE

The General Assembly of North Carolina do enact:

SECTION 1. That for the purpose of promoting greater loyalty and respect to the State and inasmuch as a special act of the Legislature has adopted an emblem of our government known as the North Carolina

State flag, that it is meet and proper that it shall be given greater prominence.

SEC. 2. That the board of trustees or managers of the several state institutions and public buildings shall provide a North Carolina flag, of such dimensions and materials as they deem best, and the same shall be displayed from a staff upon the top of each and every such building at all times except during inclement weather, and upon the death of any State officer or any prominent citizen the flag shall be put at half-mast until the burial of such person shall have taken place.

SEC. 3. That the Board of County Commissioners of the several counties in this State shall likewise authorize the procuring of a North Carolina flag, to be displayed either on a staff upon the top, or draped behind the Judge's stand, in each and every court-house in the State, and that the State flag shall be displayed at each and every term of court held, and on such other public occasions as the Commissioners may deem proper.

SEC. 4. That no State flag shall be allowed in or over any building here mentioned that does not conform to section five thousand three hundred and twenty-one of the Revisal of one thousand nine hundred and five.

SEC. 5. That this act shall be in force from and after its ratification.

In the General Assembly read three times, and ratified this 9th day of March, A.D. 1907.

THE STATE SALUTE TO THE NORTH CAROLINA FLAG

On April 25, 2007, the General Assembly of North Carolina, "for the purpose of promoting greater loyalty and respect to the State of North Carolina," adopted an official salute to the state flag: "I salute the flag of North Carolina and pledge to the Old North State love, loyalty, and faith" (G.S. 144-8).

THE STATE COLORS

The General Assembly of 1945 declared red and blue, of the shades appearing in the North Carolina state flag and the American flag, as the official state colors (G.S. 144-6).

THE MECKLENBURG DECLARATION

The Mecklenburg Declaration of May 20, 1775, has been a source of controversy among historians who have debated the Declaration's authenticity. The first argument against its historical accuracy is the lack of original documentation. The extant text of the Declaration was recalled from memory in 1800 by John McKnitt Alexander, one of the attending delegates, whose original minutes of the meeting had been lost in a fire. Secondly, the Mecklenburg Resolves, adopted just eleven days after the Mecklenburg Declaration, are comparatively weak in tone, almost to the point of being completely opposite. Many historians find it difficult to believe that the irreconcilable tone of the Declaration could have been the work of the same people who produced the Resolves.

Because of these arguments, many North Carolinians have questioned the legitimacy of having the date "May 20th 1775" on the state flag. Efforts have been made to remove the date from both the flag and the state seal, but so far these efforts have proved fruitless.

Below is the text of the Mecklenburg Declaration as it appears in volume IX, pages 1263–1265, of the *Colonial Records of North Carolina.*

The Mecklenburg Declaration of 20th May, 1775

OFFICERS
Abraham Alexander, Chairman
John McKnitt Alexander

DELEGATES

Col. Thomas Polk	Ezra Alexander	Waightsill Avery
Ephraim Brevard	William Graham	Benjamin Patton
Hezekiah J. Balch	John Quary	Mathew McClure
John Phifer	Abraham Alexander	Neil Morrison
James Harris	John McKnitt Alexander	Robert Irwin
William Kennon	Hezekiah Alexander	John Flenniken
John Ford	Adam Alexander	David Reese
Richard Barry	Charles Alexander	Richard Harris, Sen.
Henry Downs	Zacheus Wilson, Sen.	

The following resolutions were presented:

1. Resolved That whosoever directly or indirectly abetted or in any way form or manner countenanced the unchartered and dangerous invasion of our rights as claimed by Great Britain is an enemy to this country, to America, and to the inherent and inalienable rights of man.

2. Resolved That we citizens of Mecklenburg County, do hereby dissolve the political bonds which have connected us to the mother country and hereby absolve ourselves from all allegiance to the British Crown and abjure all political connections contract or association with that nation who have wantonly trampled on our rights and liberties and inhumanly shed the blood of American patriots at Lexington.

3. Resolved That we do hereby declare ourselves a free and independent people, are, and of right ought to be a sovereign and self-governing association under the control of no power other than that of our God and the General Government of the Congress to the maintenance of which independence we solemnly pledge to each other our mutual cooperation, our lives, our fortunes, and our most sacred honor.

4. Resolved That as we now acknowledge the existence and control of no law or legal officer, civil or military within this County, we do hereby ordain and adopt as a rule of life all, each and every of our former laws—wherein nevertheless the Crown of Great Britain never can be considered as holding rights, privileges, immunities, or authority therein.

5. Resolved That it is further decreed that all, each and every Military Officer in this County is hereby reinstated in his former command and authority, he acting comformably to these regulations. And that every member present of this delegation shall henceforth be a civil officer, viz., a justice of the peace, in the character of a "committee man" to issue process, hear and determine all matters of controversy according to said adopted laws and to preserve peace, union and harmony in said county, and to use every exertion to spread the love of Country and fire of freedom throughout America, until a more general and organized government be established in this Province.

THE STATE MOTTO

The General Assembly of 1893 adopted the words "Esse Quam Videri" as the state's motto, and directed that these words and the date "20 May, 1775," be placed with our coat of arms upon the Great Seal of the state (G.S. 144-2). The words "Esse Quam Videri" mean "to be rather than to seem."

Nearly every state has adopted a motto, generally in Latin because it is far more condensed and terse than the English.

Many are curious to learn the origin of our state motto. The words are found in chapter 26 of an essay entitiled, "De Amicitia" ("On Friendship") by Marcus Tillius Cicero, a Roman orator, lawyer, and philosopher who lived from 106 to 43 B.C. The chapter discusses, in part, the nature of truthful and virtuous friendship.

It is somewhat unique that from its declaration of independence until the act of 1893, North Carolina had no motto. It was one of the few states that did not have a motto and the only one of the original thirteen without one.

THE STATE TOAST

The following toast was officially adopted as the state toast of North Carolina by the General Assembly of 1957 (G.S. 149-2).

Here's to the land of the long leaf pine,
The summer land where the sun doth shine,
Where the weak grow strong, and the strong grow great,
Here's to "Down Home," the Old North State!

Here's to the land of the cotton bloom white,
Where the scuppernong perfumes the breeze at night,
Where the soft southern moss and jessamine mate,
Neath the murmuring pines of the Old North State!

Here's to the land where the galax grows,
Where the rhododendron's rosette glows,
Where soars Mount Mitchell's summit great,
In the "Land of the Sky," in the Old North State!

Here's to the land where maidens are fair,
Where friends are true and cold hearts rare,
The near land, the dear land, whatever fate,
The blest land, the best land, the Old North State!

THE STATE SONG

"The Old North State" was adopted as the official song of the state of North Carolina by the General Assembly of 1927 (G.S. 149-1). The composer, New Bern, North Carolina, native William Joseph Gaston (1778-1844), was a highly respected lawyer, legislator, congressman, and jurist. He wrote the words in 1840 while in Raleigh for a session of the supreme court. At the Whig state convention in October of that year, the song was performed publicly for the first time.

Illustration by Duane Raver. Reproduced by permission of the artist.

THE STATE FLOWER

The General Assembly of 1941 designated the dogwood (*Cornus florida*) as the state flower (G.S. 145-1).

The dogwood is one of the most prevalent trees in North Carolina and can be found in all parts of the state from the mountains to the coast. Its blossoms, which appear in early spring and continue into summer, are most often found in white, although shades of pink are not uncommon.

THE STATE BIRD

The cardinal was selected by popular choice as our state bird on March 4, 1943 (G.S. 145-2).

The cardinal (*Cardinalis cardinalis*) is sometimes called the winter redbird because it is most noticeable during the winter when it is the only "redbird" present. A year-round resident of North Carolina, the cardinal is one of the most common birds in our gardens, meadows, and woodlands. The male cardinal is red all over except for the area of its throat and the region around its bill, which are black; it is eight to nine inches long, about the size of a gray catbird only with a longer tail. The head is conspicuously crested, and the large stout bill is red. The female is buff-brown with the red confined mostly to the crest, wings, and tail. This difference in coloring is common among many birds. Because it is the female that sits on the nest, her coloring must blend more with her natural surroundings to protect her eggs and young from predators. There are no seasonal changes in her plumage.

The cardinal is a fine singer, and what is unusual is that the female sings as beautifully as the male. The male generally monopolizes the art of song in the bird world. They can be heard at any time of year.

The nest of the cardinal is rather an untidy affair built of twigs, leaves, and plant fibers, and is found in low shrubs, small trees, or thickets. Cardinals inhabit woodland edges, thickets, brushy swamps, and gardens. The usual number of eggs set is three to four; they are pale green with red-brown spots.

By nature, the cardinal is a seedeater, but does not dislike small fruits and insects, and often visits feeders during winter.

Illustration by Duane Raver. Reproduced by permission of the artist.

THE STATE TREE

The pine (genus *Pinus*) was officially designated as the state tree by the General Assembly of 1963 (G.S. 145-3).

The pine is the most common of the trees found in North Carolina, as well as the most important one in the history of our state. During the colonial and early statehood periods, the pine was a vital part of the economy of North Carolina. From it came many of the "naval stores"—resin, turpentine, and timber—needed by merchants and the navy for their ships. The pine has continued to supply North Carolina with many important wood products, particularly in the building industry.

THE STATE MAMMAL

The General Assembly of 1969 designated the gray squirrel as the official state mammal (G.S. 145-5).

Of North Carolina's four squirrel species, the gray squirrel (*Sciurus carolinensis*) is the most common. These bushy-tailed, acrobatic climbers are most abundant in hardwood forests where trees provide both nuts (mast) for food and cavities for protection against enemies and foul weather; they also flourish in urban and suburban woodlots. Although not as secure against predators nor as protective against the elements, nests constructed of leaves are the squirrel's alternative dwelling when tree cavities are less numerous or infested with pests.

Nuts, particularly acorns, fruits, and seeds, constitute the bulk of the gray squirrel's diet. It appears that in years when nuts are abundant, squirrels survive winter in larger numbers and females produce larger litters of young. Conversely, when such food is less abundant, the survivors are in poorer health and reproduce less.

Late winter and early spring litters are born in February and March, and summer litters in July or August. The size of the litter ranges between one and six young, with the average being 2.5.

Illustration by Duane Raver. Reproduced by permission of the artist.

THE STATE SHELL

The General Assembly of 1965 designated the Scotch bonnet (pronounced *bonay*) (*Phalium granulatum*) as the state shell (G.S. 145-4).

A beautifully shaped shell, the Scotch bonnet's colors range from white to yellowish-white with yellow to brown-colored squares or spiral bands. The two-to-four-inch shell is produced by a gastropod, a marine snail, that lives on sand in moderately shallow water. Divers and commercial fishermen frequently find live specimens offshore at depths between fifty and one hundred fifty feet. It is rare, however, to see live specimens on shore unless a storm washes them onto the beach.

According to the North Carolina Wildlife Resources Commission, the Scotch bonnet is so named for its resemblance to a woolen cap worn by Scottish peasants, and its adoption as a state symbol honors our early Scottish settlers.

THE STATE SALTWATER FISH

The General Assembly of 1971 designated the channel bass (red drum) as the official state saltwater fish (G.S. 145-6).

Red drum (*Sciaenops ocellatus*) exist in varying numbers from year to year in Tar Heel coastal waters, and channel bass, as the larger of the red drum fish are known, have been found to weigh up to seventy-five pounds and measure up to five feet long. The scales on older specimens are approximately the size of guitar picks. The fish's blunt snout has a mouth that is well adapted to feeding on the ocean bottom. Favored foods include other fish, shrimp, crabs, and sand dollars.

Illustration by Duane Raver. Reproduced by permission of the artist.

THE STATE INSECT

The General Assembly of 1973 designated the honeybee (*Apis mellifera*) as the official state insect (G.S. 145-7).

Europeans brought the honeybee to North America in the 1600s. This industrious creature produced $780,000 worth of honey in 2006. Honey is made from the nectar of sourwood flowers. However, the greatest value of honeybees is their role in the growing cycle as a major contributor to the pollination of North Carolina crops.

THE STATE PRECIOUS STONE

The General Assembly of 1973 designated the emerald as the official state precious stone (G.S. 145-8).

North Carolina is home to a rich diversity of minerals such as sapphires, rubies, garnets, diamonds, and emeralds. This great assortment of minerals includes some of the most valuable and unique emeralds in the world. One of the most famous, the "Carolina Emerald," now owned by Tiffany & Company of New York, was found at Hiddenite,

(*Left*) The "Empress Caroline." (*Right*) The "Carolina Queen." Both photographs by Alan Westmoreland, courtesy of the North Carolina Office of Archives and History, and R. Gregory Jewelers, Inc.

near Statesville, in 1970. When cut to 13.14 carats, the stone was valued at the time at $100,000 and was the largest and finest cut emerald on this continent. More recently, in 1998, well-known emerald miner James Hill found at North American Emerald Mines at Hiddenite a 71-carat rough emerald that was cut into the 7.85 carat "Carolina Prince" and the 18.88 carat "Carolina Queen." The oval-shaped "Carolina Prince" sold for $500,000 to a private collector. The pear-shaped "Carolina Queen," owned by a consortium of investors, is considered by some experts as even more fine and important than the "Carolina Emerald." Its owners believe it could sell for as much as one million dollars. Also part of the 1998 discovery was the 858-carat "Empress Caroline" (formerly known as the "Jolly Green Giant"), an emerald of deep color and fine quality. Its owners plan to keep it uncut and offer it for exhibition.

For many years, the record for the largest rough emerald ever discovered in North Carolina was 1,438 carats. Its source, Hiddenite, has since yielded even more spectacular finds. In 1985, a 1,686-carat rough emerald crystal was found, but it was dwarfed by a high-quality crystal estimated at 1,861.9 carats, a specimen unearthed in December 2003 in three large, separate, but perfectly matched, pieces and a chip. This latest reconstructed emerald is the largest ever reported in North America.

Illustration by Duane Raver. Reproduced by permission of the artist.

THE STATE REPTILE

The General Assembly of 1979 adopted the turtle as the state reptile, designating the eastern box turtle (*Terrapene carolina*) as the emblem representing the turtles inhabiting North Carolina (G.S. 145-9).

The eastern box turtle is the species of North American land turtles native to the southern Appalachian Mountains. They live mostly in or near wooded areas, and eat a variety of plants and animals such as berries, mushrooms, slugs, and insects. When picked up, the turtle usually does not try to bite, but rather draws in its head, feet, and tail, closing its hinged shell tightly. In June or July, the female lays three to six eggs in a hole that she has dug with her hind legs, then covers them with soil where they remain until hatched about two to three months later. An adult is about five or six inches in length and can live in the wild for approximately forty years.

Photograph courtesy of the North Carolina Granite Corporation.

THE STATE ROCK

The General Assembly of 1979 designated granite as the official rock for the state of North Carolina (G.S. 145-10).

The state of North Carolina has been blessed with an abundant source of "the noble rock," granite. Just outside Mount Airy in Surry County is the largest open-faced granite quarry in the world, measuring one mile long and one-half mile wide—big enough to be seen from outer space by astronauts circling the earth! Each year, it produces over 2,000,000 feet of Mount Airy White (Caesar White). The granite from this quarry is unblemished, gleaming, and without interfering seams to mar its splendor. The high quality of this granite allows its widespread use as a building material, in both industrial and laboratory applications where super smooth surfaces are necessary.

North Carolina granite has been used for many significant edifices of government throughout the United States such as the Wright Brothers Memorial at Kitty Hawk, the gold depository at Fort Knox, the Arlington Memorial Bridge, and numerous courthouses throughout the land. It is fitting and just that the state recognize granite for providing employment to its citizens and enhancing the beauty of its public buildings.

Aerial view of Mount Airy Quarry. Photograph courtesy of the North Carolina Granite Corporation.

THE STATE BEVERAGE

The General Assembly of 1987 adopted milk as the official state beverage (G.S. 145-10.1).

In making milk the official state beverage, North Carolina followed many other states including our northern neighbor, Virginia, and Wisconsin.

In 2006, North Carolina ranked thirty-first among milk producing states in the nation; California and Wisconsin ranked first and second, respectively. There were 375 commercial dairy farmers in the state as of January 1, 2004, producing 121 million gallons of milk during the previous year. The North Carolina Department of Agriculture and Consumer Services reports that our cash receipts for the sale of milk by dairy farmers amounted to over $138 million in 2006.

THE STATE HISTORICAL BOAT

The General Assembly of 1987 adopted the shad boat as the official state historical boat (G.S. 145-11).

The shad boat was developed on Roanoke Island and is known for its unique crafting and maneuverability. The name is derived from that of the fish it was used to catch—the shad.

Traditional small sailing craft were generally ill-suited to the waterways and weather conditions along the coast. The shallow draft of the shad boat plus its speed and easy handling made the boat ideal for the upper sounds where the water was shallow and the weather changed rapidly. The boats were built using native trees such as cypress, juniper, and white cedar, and varied in length between twenty-two and thirty-three feet. Construction was so expensive that production of the shad boat ended in the 1930s, although it was widely used into the 1950s. The boats were so well constructed that some, nearly one hundred years old, are still seen around Manteo and Hatteras.

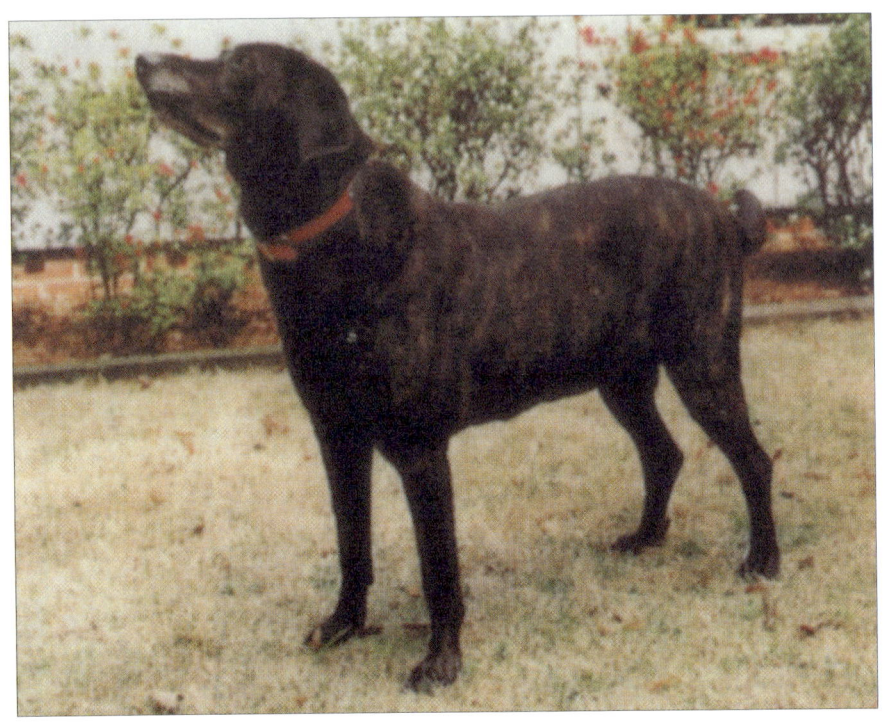

From the *North Carolina Manual*, 2001-2002.

THE STATE DOG

The Plott hound was officially adopted as our state dog on August 12, 1989 (G.S. 145-13).

The Plott hound breed originated in the mountains of North Carolina around 1750 and is the only breed known to have originated in this state. Named for German immigrant Johannes George Plott, who developed the breed as a wild boar hound, the Plott hound is a legendary hunting dog known as a courageous fighter and tenacious tracker. He is also a gentle and extremely loyal companion to hunters of North Carolina. The Plott hound is very quick of foot with superior instincts and has always been a favorite of big-game hunters.

The Plott hound has a beautiful brindle-colored coat and a spine-tingling, bugle-like call. It is also one of only four breeds known to be of American origin.

Photograph courtesy of the Scottish Tartans Museum, Franklin, North Carolina.

THE STATE TARTAN

The General Assembly of 1991 adopted the Carolina tartan as the official tartan of the state of North Carolina (G.S. 145-15).

Tartan, a plaid textile design consisting of stripes of varying width and color, was first made famous by Scottish Highlanders. The earliest sample of tartan found in Scotland is the "Falkirk tartan," which dates from ca. 250 A.D. It is housed in the Museum of Scotland in Edinburgh.

The St. Andrew's Societies of North and South Carolina, organizations that celebrate and promote Scottish heritage, approved of the design for a Carolina tartan proposed to them by textile historian and tartan weaver, Peter MacDonald of Crieff, Scotland. The Scottish Tartans Society, a group of tartan historians organized in 1963 to encourage research into tartan and Highland dress, recorded the Carolina tartan in its database in 1981. Also officially adopted by South Carolina, the Carolina tartan is a variation of a tartan associated with King Charles II whose 1663 land grant resulted in the creation of the Carolina colony.

Scottish families began settling in both North and South Carolina in the late 1600s. Throughout the first half of the eighteenth century, large numbers of Highland Scots and Ulster Scots settled in the two Carolinas, becoming a vital part of both colonies. The adoption of the Carolina tartan recognizes the desire of many North Carolina citizens of Scottish descent to honor their ancestral ties.

Courtesy of the North Carolina Department of Agriculture and Consumer Services.

THE STATE VEGETABLE

The General Assembly of 1995 adopted the sweet potato (*Ipomocea batatas*) as the official vegetable of the state of North Carolina (G.S. 145–17).

As part of an assignment, students at a Wilson County school petitioned the North Carolina General Assembly to establish the sweet potato as the official state vegetable, and a new state symbol was born. In 2006, North Carolina growers produced over 43 percent of the nation's sweet potatoes, with 7,020 hundredweights (cwt) harvested on approximately 39,000 acres of land.

Sweet potatoes are sometimes confused with yams, which originated in West Africa and Asia. The confusion dates from the days of the slave trade, when slaves from Africa mistook the sweet potato with the nyami of their native land. The word yam comes from this African word. What's more, for many years, the sweet potato industry has marketed certain varieties of sweet potatoes as yams. These boast a vivid orange color, a soft, moist consistency when cooked, and a uniquely sweet flavor. Other varieties of sweet potatoes, however, are lighter skinned and have a firmer, drier texture when cooked. True yams also tend to be dry and starchy, but are rough and scaly instead of smooth and thin–skinned like sweet potatoes.

The very nutritious sweet potato is low in fat and high in vitamins A and C.

Photograph courtesy of the North Carolina Grape Council.

THE STATE FRUIT

The General Assembly of 2001 named the scuppernong grape the official state fruit (G.S. 145-18).

The scuppernong is a bronze variety of muscadine grape (*Vitis rotundifolia*) native to North Carolina and has the distinction of being the first grape ever actively cultivated in the United States. It was named for the Scuppernong River, which rises in Washington County and flows to the Albemarle Sound. Giovanni da Verrazano noticed this variety as far back as 1524, and English explorers reported on the grapes to Queen Elizabeth and Sir Walter Raleigh in the 1580s. The explorers described the barrier islands of what is now, in part, Roanoke Island, as full of grapes and the soil of the land as "so abounding with sweet trees that bring rich and most pleasant gummes, grapes of such greatness, yet wild, as France, Spain, nor Italy hath not greater." The Roanoke colonists are credited with discovering the scuppernong "Mother Vineyard," a vine that is now over four hundred years old and covers half an acre.

By 2006, 495 acres of bronze muscadines and 115 acres of black muscadines had been planted in North Carolina. In fact, cultivation of many grape varieties is a small but growing part of the North Carolina economy. The value of the 2006 grape crop exceeded $4.6 million, and in that same year, according to the North Carolina Department of Commerce, there were 350 vineyards and 55 wineries located throughout the state.

THE STATE BERRIES

Courtesy of the North Carolina Department of Agriculture and Consumer Services.

In 2001, the General Assembly named the strawberry as the official red berry of North Carolina, and named the blueberry as the official blue berry of the state (G.S. 145-18).

Both strawberries and blueberries are very important to the agricultural economy of the state. In 2006, strawberries brought in over nineteen million dollars while blueberries generated nearly forty-nine million dollars. According to the North Carolina Department of Agriculture and Consumer Services (NCDACS), our state ranks third in the nation for strawberries harvested, and is unique in that it sells almost all of its crops fresh here at home. Harvest season runs from early April to mid-June. Not far behind in the growing season are blueberries, available from mid-May through August. NCDACS also reports that we rank behind only four other states in the production of blueberries.

Not only are these berries sweet and delicious to eat, they also provide important nutrients as well. Strawberries (genus *Fragaria*) are high in vitamins A and C, and a one-cup serving supplies 8 percent of the recommended daily allowance (RDA) of iron. A cup of blueberries (genus *Vaccinium*) supplies 50 percent of the RDA of vitamin C, as well as 22 percent of the fiber recommended for a healthy diet.

Courtesy of the North Carolina Department of Agriculture and Consumer Services.

Strawberries and blueberries are grown throughout North Carolina, and consumers can pick their own berries at farms across the state. A list of these farms is provided by the NCDACS on its website.

Photograph by Larry Allain. Courtesy of the United States Geological Survey.

THE STATE WILDFLOWER

In 2003, the General Assembly designated the Carolina lily (*Lilium michauxii*) as the official state wildflower (G.S. 145-20).

Named for the French botanist, André Michaux, a noted eighteenth-century naturalist and explorer, this perennial flower grows throughout the state, from the forests and hills of Cherokee County to the coastal pocosins of Hyde and Pamlico counties. The stem can grow up to four feet high, and can have up to six flowers at the summit, though one to three are more common. This nodding flower's petals are brilliant red-orange with brown spots, and arched back so that the tips overlap near the top of the stem.

The Carolina lily grows throughout the Southeast, from West Virginia to Florida, and can bloom as late as October, though it is most prevalent in July and August.

Courtesy of the North Carolina Plant Conservation Program.

THE STATE CARNIVOROUS PLANT

The Venus flytrap (*Dionaea muscipula*) was adopted as the official state carnivorous plant by the General Assembly in 2005 (G.S. 145-22).

Native only to an area within an approximately ninety-mile radius of Wilmington, North Carolina, within the coastal plain of North and South Carolina, the insect-eating Venus flytrap is protected as a "species of special concern" by state law: collecting wild specimens from public land, or even from private land without permission, is illegal. Fines per violation can run from hundreds to thousands of dollars. Commercial growers or others with special permission, however, are permitted to offer their plants for sale. In North Carolina, only seventy-five viable populations of the small flowering perennial plant exist in eleven of our counties. Development of farm and timberland threatens the flytrap's already limited natural habitat, but poachers are also a major concern. In an effort to protect the plant from poachers, the North Carolina Department of Agriculture and Consumer Services and The Nature Conservancy have begun a program to mark wild specimens so that inspectors can identify plants dug from public lands.

Hinged lobes at the ends of the Venus flytrap's leaves are fringed with finger-like edges. When at least two of the tiny trigger hairs inside these lobes are vibrated in succession, the trap snaps shut in under a second, capturing its prey. Scientists do not understand the exact mechanism by which this occurs. Gradually the edges of the lobes seal together, and enzymes are secreted to digest the food, which provide the plant with nutrients. Digestion takes several days, and when the trap reopens, the remaining exoskeleton is either blown away by the wind or washed away by rain. After eating about three or four insects, the individual trap will die, but the larger plant will live on. Sometimes the individual traps will also die after catching an insect that is too big for it to digest.

THE STATE DANCES

The General Assembly of 2005 adopted clogging as the official folk dance of North Carolina and shagging as the official popular dance of North Carolina (G.S. 145-24).

Both clogging and shagging have a long history here, are beloved by many, and performed at competitions and events across the state. Clogging is a traditional American folk dance that evolved from European, African, and Native American folk dances. It originated in the southern Appalachian Mountains and is accompanied by traditional string music of the same area. Today, clogging has come to enjoy both national and international popularity. America's Clogging Hall of Fame (ACHF) at the Stompin' Grounds in Maggie Valley, North Carolina works to preserve the history and heritage of this dance by sponsoring competitions, awarding scholarships, and inducting influential dancers into its Hall of Fame.

Unlike flatfoot and buck dancers, cloggers frequently use taps on their shoes to accentuate the rhythm of their steps. Although clogging developed primarily as an individual expressive dance, groups of cloggers

The famed Apple Chill Cloggers unveiled a new routine for the "Family Days: Mountains of North Carolina" program by the North Carolina Museum of History on April 23, 2005.

sometimes choreograph their routines so that the steps are performed in unison. Clogging's distinct footwork involves high kicks and combinations of striking the dancing surface with the heels, toes, and balls of the feet.

While clogging is generally associated with the mountains, shagging conjures images of the beaches and oceanside pavilions. Shag contests were mentioned in the *Wilmington Morning Star* as early as 1932, having already been introduced there in 1928. That early shag was based on the Charleston and foxtrot, according to its Wilmington inventor, and became all the rage at colleges and resorts throughout the South and mid–Atlantic. Modern shag, on the other hand, is quite different in its style and basic form. It was originally danced to the jump blues and transitional swing of the 1940s, which by 1949 had become rhythm and blues. In North Carolina, unique sub-styles have evolved in urban areas, at resort centers, and on college campuses from Atlantic Beach to Charlotte, including Carolina Beach, Raleigh, Durham, Greensboro, and Winston-Salem. Although today's shagging can be more coordinated, smooth steps are important no matter what the style.

Early on, shag dancing was considered by some to be a bit scandalous, and teenagers caught up in the phenomenon were compelled to sneak off for a night of dancing. In the 1960s and 1970s, "Beach Bands" emerged, playing the beach music that has become so associated with shagging. Both the dance and the music are still popular—shag contests and clubs are plentiful, and some radio stations are devoted entirely to beach music.

John Hook contributed to this article.

Above: A young couple dances in a Nags Head beach club in August 1948.
Below: Walter and Elmyra Upchurch shag with flair at Loafers Beach Club. Photograph by Rickie Lipscomb. Courtesy of Loafers Beach Club in Raleigh, North Carolina.

Photograph courtesy of the North Carolina Christmas Tree Association.

THE STATE CHRISTMAS TREE

The Fraser fir (*Abies fraseri*) was adopted as the official Christmas tree of North Carolina in 2005 (G.S. 145-25).

Favored for its deep green color, long-lasting aroma, exceptional needle retention, and strong branches that support heavier ornaments, the Fraser fir is the most popular variety of Christmas tree around the country. In fact, high quality North Carolina grown Fraser fir Christmas trees have been chosen to grace the Blue Room of the White House ten times, most recently in 2007. According to the North Carolina Department of Agriculture and Consumer Services (NCDACS), our state supplied $105 million worth (21.2 percent) of this demand, and we rank second in the nation behind Oregon for number of Christmas trees harvested. Currently, over 50 million trees are being tended by 16,000 growers on 25,000 acres. More than 90 percent of all Christmas trees grown in North Carolina are Fraser firs. A typical six- to seven-foot-tall Fraser has been visited by its grower over 100 times and has been developing for approximately twelve years. If left to mature, a tree can grow as high as 80 feet, with a trunk diameter of up to one and a half feet!

Named for Scottish botanist John Fraser, these beautiful trees are native to the southern Appalachians, which Fraser explored in the late 1700s. The cool temperatures and abundant rainfall above 4,500 feet, where the firs are naturally found, create the ideal conditions for growth, yet most tree farms are located at lower elevations. Fraser firs are thriving on these farms, but they are susceptible to damage there and in their natural habitat, particularly from the balsam woolly adelgid, an insect native to Europe. First discovered on Mount Mitchell in 1957, the balsam woolly adelgid has since destroyed approximately 90 percent of Fraser firs in the wild, and they cost growers over $1.5 million a year in pest control. Because of the Fraser fir's ecological and economic importance to the state, researchers are always seeking new and effective treatments to keep trees healthy.

The 2007 official White House Christmas tree on display in the Blue Room was an 18-foot Fraser fir grown at Mistletoe Meadows tree farm in Laurel Springs, North Carolina. Photograph courtesy of Mistletoe Meadows.

THE STATE FRESHWATER TROUT

In 2005, the General Assembly adopted the southern Appalachian strain of brook trout (*Salvelinus fontinalis*) as the official freshwater trout of the State of North Carolina (G.S. 145-26).

Two strains of brook trout live in North Carolina streams: the northern and southern strains. Both are greenish brown with light red spots and a reddish orange color along their bellies and lower fins, have dark wavy lines on their backs, and sport white-edged fins and tails. The belly color often intensifies during fall spawning. While the strains look identical, the southern one is genetically distinct. These beautiful fish prefer cool, clear water that is well oxygenated and eat a varied diet, including insects, crustaceans, and frogs. They generally live about four years and average six to eight inches in length. Because brook trout are highly sensitive to pollutants such as acid rain and chemical runoff, scientists look to them as indicators of water quality.

Known by several nicknames—"specks," "brookie," and "speckle" or "speckled" trout—brook trout are a favorite catch of anglers and can be fished using a variety of techniques and baits, including fly fishing for wild trout and spin casting, worms, and corn for hatchery-reared trout. Their popularity contributes to recreational tourism, and thus, to economic development. Moreover, they are historically and culturally important to western North Carolina, representing to many the unspoiled mountain settings that are so highly prized today.

Illustration by Duane Raver. Courtesy of the U.S. Fish and Wildlife Service.

OFFICIAL MILITARY ACADEMY

The General Assembly of 1991 adopted the Oak Ridge Military Academy as the official state military academy (G.S. 145-14).

Oak Ridge Military Academy, in Oak Ridge, North Carolina, is a military and college preparatory academy for young men and women in grades seven through twelve. Established in 1852 as a Society of Friends school for boys, Oak Ridge is the third oldest military school in the United States. It became the first military academy in the United States to admit female cadets in 1971. As a testament to the quality of the curriculum and the student body, one hundred percent of the academy's graduating seniors have been accepted to the college or university of their choice since the early 1990s. Most cadets live on campus, and all enjoy a variety of traditional school activities such as athletics, pep rallies, dances, field trips, and informal recreation.

Oak Ridge's mission statement reads:

> The mission of Oak Ridge Military Academy, a college preparatory school, is to provide an educational environment which stimulates curiosity, fosters scholarly competence, encourages academic excellence, rewards self-discipline, and develops leadership potential through student involvement in both the curricular and co-curricular educational process.
>
> The military dimension of Oak Ridge Military Academy's program seeks to reinforce every other aspect of the mission and to add a set of values which can be applied throughout life, including a work ethic, a sense of responsibility, integrity, morality, all of which are intended to instill and preserve shared beliefs in the principles that have made our society and our country great.

All cadets are required to adhere to the provisions of the cadet honor code and creed. The cadet honor code pledges, "I will not lie, cheat, steal, or tolerate those who do," and the cadet creed asserts, "I will be honest and courteous, respect the rights and dignity of others, and be proud of how I act and who I am."

Courtesy of the North Carolina Department of Agriculture and Consumer Services.

OFFICIAL WATERMELON FESTIVALS

In 1993, the North Carolina General Assembly adopted two official watermelon festivals (G.S. 145-16).

The Hertford County Watermelon Festival is the official northeastern North Carolina watermelon festival and is observed annually during the last four days of the first week in August. The Fair Bluff Watermelon Festival is the official southeastern North Carolina watermelon festival and is observed annually in mid-July.

Watermelons are usually harvested in our state from June through August. This sweet and refreshing treat is 92 percent water and a particularly good source of lycopene and vitamins A and C.

OFFICIAL INTERNATIONAL FESTIVAL

In 2003, the North Carolina General Assembly designated Folkmoot USA as the official state international festival (G.S. 145-19).

Folkmoot USA is an international folk festival held each summer in western North Carolina at the entrance to the Great Smoky Mountains National Park. Sporting colorful costumes and playing unique instruments, folk dancers and musicians from around the world share their cultural heritage with locals and tourists alike. Most of the work of the festival is carried out by the more than six hundred volunteers who assist annually.

OFFICIAL AIRPORTS AND MUSEUMS

In 2003, the General Assembly designated the Asheboro Municipal Airport as the official location of the North Carolina Aviation Hall of Fame and the North Carolina Aviation Museum. The Wilmington International Airport was designated as the official location of the North Carolina Museum of Aviation (G.S. 145-21).

OFFICIAL STATE TRADITIONAL POTTERY BIRTHPLACE

In 2005, the General Assembly designated the Seagrove area as the official location of the birthplace of North Carolina traditional pottery (G.S. 145-23).

The small town of Seagrove in southern Randolph County has a population of fewer than three hundred, but it and the surrounding area draw thousands of visitors each year in search of beautiful pottery. What is referred to as the "Seagrove area" includes portions of Randolph, Chatham, Moore, and Montgomery counties. Here, ever since the eighteenth century, potters have fashioned the local clays into a variety of wares, both functional and fanciful. Early pieces were more utilitarian stoneware, such as milk crocks, whiskey jugs, and jars. As the need for these sorts of objects faded, potters adapted to a new market. Around 1920, they began crafting more artistic pieces for the vacationers at nearby Pinehurst who came shopping for collectibles. This evolution produced items such as vases, pitchers, and other decorative items. Jacques and Juliana Busbee, founders of Jugtown Pottery in 1917, were also instrumental in promoting the local potters' work nationwide.

Some of the early families associated with North Carolina's traditional pottery include the Chriscoe, Cole, Craven, Luck, McNeill, Owen, and Teague families. Indeed, some Seagrove potters represent the eighth and ninth generation of potters in their families. Both the North Carolina Pottery Center and the Museum of North Carolina Traditional Pottery are dedicated to preserving and educating the public about North Carolina's pottery tradition. One might also attend the annual Seagrove Pottery Festival, which is always held on the Saturday and Sunday before Thanksgiving. It is an excellent opportunity to see demonstrations, participate in an auction, and shop from most of the area's over ninety potters who exhibit there.

Seagrove potter Philmore Graves in his workshop (ca. 1930s). Photograph courtesy of the Museum of North Carolina Traditional Pottery.

OFFICIAL COLLARD FESTIVAL

The General Assembly of 2007 adopted the Ayden Collard Festival as the official collard festival of North Carolina (G.S. 145-27).

In 1975, as a way to celebrate its agricultural heritage, the town of Ayden, in Pitt County, decided to hold a festival. Citizens were invited to choose a name by casting ballots that were printed in the local newspaper, and by a wide margin, the Collard Festival was born. A variety of events is always offered, including pageants, musical and dance performances, sports contests, rides, and crafts. Naturally, the festival hosts both a collard cooking and collard eating contest! Sponsored by the Town of Ayden and various businesses, and supported by hundreds of volunteers, the annual festivities are held during the first week of September, from the Tuesday after Labor Day through Saturday.

Collards are a favorite food in the southern United States. They are usually simmered with salt pork or ham hock for seasoning; red pepper flakes and vinegar are also favorite accompaniments. A New Year's Day tradition is to eat a special meal said to bring prosperity and good luck.

Typically, the menu consists of pork, black-eyed peas, cornbread, and greens—the greens being a symbol of folding money. The nutrients that come from collards are reason enough to eat them year round: they are an especially good source of calcium, fiber, and vitamins A, C, and K.

Pile of collard greens for sale at the State Farmers Market.

OFFICIAL FOOD FESTIVAL OF PIEDMONT TRIAD REGION

The General Assembly of 2007 adopted the Lexington Barbecue Festival as the official food festival of the North Carolina Piedmont Triad region (G.S. 145-28).

The first annual Lexington Barbecue Festival was held on October 27, 1984, with an estimated 30,000 attendees enjoying the 3,000 pounds of barbecue prepared for the inaugural event. Ten years later, over

"King 'Que" sand sculpture created for the 2007 Lexington Barbecue Festival. Photograph courtesy of the Lexington *Dispatch*.

100,000 people feasted on 11,000 pounds of the slow cooked, hickory smoked pork shoulder basted with a distinct mixture of vinegar, ketchup, water, salt, and pepper (a concoction known as "dip"). By 2003, an estimated 150,000 visitors flocked to Uptown Lexington, a testament to the continued popularity of the event.

Delicious food is certainly the highlight of the festival, but is not the only attraction. Sand sculptures, juried arts and crafts, various entertainers, and racing pigs are merely a sampling of the fun to be had. Moreover, October has been dubbed "Barbecue Month" by the City of Lexington and Davidson County: various pig-themed athletic tournaments and contests are held in the run-up to the festival day, which was named One of the Top Ten Food Festivals in the Country by *Travel and Leisure* magazine and a Top 20 Event for the Month of October by the Southeast Tourism Society in 2002, 2006, and 2007. Participants can enter the Tour de Pig cycling event, the Hawg Run, or perhaps a "Pig Tale" writing competition, to name a few.

The Lexington Barbecue Festival is held on one of the last two Saturdays in October each year, and admission is free.

OFFICIAL COMMUNITY THEATER

In 2007, the General Assembly adopted the Thalian Association in Wilmington, North Carolina as the official community theater of North Carolina (G.S. 145-29).

Organized in 1788, and chartered by the State in 1814, the Thalian Association is the oldest community theater in North Carolina. Its official adoption honors the Association's long tradition of supporting civic and artistic activities in the community, as well as its contributions to the cultural life of this state. Notable events in the Thalian Association's history include partnering with the City of Wilmington to construct a combination public theater, library, and City Hall building, called Thalian Hall; hosting performances to raise funds for those suffering during yellow fever and smallpox epidemics; supporting the arts and education in times of economic decline and poverty; helping restore Thalian Hall to its original grandeur; introducing children's theater to Wilmington; and promoting the state's culture and history to visitors from here and abroad.

Performers from a Thalian Association production of *Cats*. Photograph courtesy of the Thalian Association.

Each year the Thalian Association stages five dramas or musicals, plus several productions of children's theater. It also hosts two major fundraising events annually: the Southern Coastal Bluegrass Festival, at Fort Fisher, North Carolina, and the Orange Street ArtsFest in Wilmington.

GOVERNORS

GOVERNORS OF "VIRGINIA"

Name	Qualified	Term
Ralph Lane	[April 9], 1585	1585-1586
John White	[April 26], 1587	1587

PROPRIETARY CHIEF EXECUTIVES

Name	Qualified	Term
(Samuel Stephens)	—	[1662-1664]
William Drummond	February 23, 1665	1665-[1667]
Samuel Stephens	—, 1667	[1667-1670]
Peter Carteret	March 10, 1670	1670-1671
Peter Carteret	—, 1671	1671-1672
John Jenkins	[May—], 1672	1672-1675
Thomas Eastchurch	October —, 1675	1675-1676
[Speaker-Assembly]	[Spring, 1676]	1676
John Jenkins	March—, 1676	1676-1677
Thomas Eastchurch	—	—
Thomas Miller	July —, 1677	1677
[Rebel Council]	December —, 1677	1677-1679
Seth Sothel	—	—
John Harvey	July —, 1679	1679
John Jenkins	December —, 1679	1679-1681
Henry Wilkinson	—	—
Seth Sothel	—, [1682]	[1682]-1689
John Archdale	December —, 1683	1683-1686
John Gibbs	November —, 1689	1689-1690
Phillip Ludwell	May —, 1690	1690-1691
Thomas Jarvis	July —, 1690	1690-1694
Phillip Ludwell	November —, 1693	1693-1695
Thomas Harvey	July —, 1694	1694-1699
John Archdale	June —, 1695	1695
John Archdale	January —, 1697	1697
Henderson Walker	July —, 1699	1699-1703
Robert Daniel	July —, 1703	1703-1705
Thomas Cary	March 21, 1705	1705-1706
William Glover	July 13, 1706	1706-1707
Thomas Cary	August —, 1707	1707
William Glover	October 28, 1707	1707-1708
Thomas Cary	July 24, 1708	1708-1711
[William Glover]	—	[1709-1710]
Edward Hyde	January 22, 1711	1711-1712
Edward Hyde	May 9, 1712	1712
Thomas Pollock	September 12, 1712	1712-1714
Charles Eden	May 28, 1714	1714-1722

Name	Qualified	Term
Thomas Pollock	March 30, 1722	1722
William Reed	September 7, 1722	1722-1724
George Burrington	January 15, 1724	1724-1725
Edward Moseley	October 31, 1724	1724
Sir Richard Everard	July 17, 1725	1725-1731

ROYAL CHIEF EXECUTIVES

Name	Qualified	Term
George Burrington	February 25, 1731	1731-1734
Nathaniel Rice	April 17, 1734	1734
Gabriel Johnston	November 2, 1734	1734-1752
Nathaniel Rice	July 17, 1752	1752-1753
Matthew Rowan	February 1, 1753	1753-1754
Arthur Dobbs	November 1, 1754	1754-1765
James Hasell	October 15, 1763	1763
William Tryon	April 3, 1765	1765
William Tryon	December 20, 1765	1765-1771
James Hasell	July 1, 1771	1771
Josiah Martin	August 12, 1771	1771-1775
James Hasell	October 8, 1774	1774

ELECTED BY THE GENERAL ASSEMBLY

Name	Residence	Qualified	Term
Richard Caswell	Dobbs	December 21, 1776	1776-1777
Richard Caswell	Dobbs	April 18, 1777	1777-1778
Richard Caswell	Dobbs	April 20, 1778	1778-1779
Richard Caswell	Dobbs	May 4, 1779	1779-1780
Abner Nash	Craven	April 21, 1780	1780-1781
Thomas Burke	Orange	June 26, 1781	1781-1782
Alexander Martin	Guilford	October 5, 1781	1781-1782
Alexander Martin	Guilford	April 22, 1782	1782-1783
Alexander Martin	Guilford	April 30, 1783	1783-1784
Alexander Martin	Guilford	May 3, 1784	1784-1785
Richard Caswell	Dobbs	May 13, 1785	1785
Richard Caswell	Dobbs	December 12, 1785	1785-1786
Richard Caswell	Dobbs	December 23, 1786	1786-1787
Samuel Johnston	Chowan	December 20, 1787	1787-1788
Samuel Johnston	Chowan	November 18, 1788	1788-1789
Samuel Johnston	Chowan	November 18, 1789	1789
Alexander Martin	Guilford	December 17, 1789	1789-1790
Alexander Martin	Guilford	December 5, 1790	1790-1792
Alexander Martin	Guilford	January 2, 1792	1792
Richard Dobbs Spaight	Craven	December 14, 1792	1792-1793
Richard Dobbs Spaight	Craven	December 26, 1793	1793-1795

Name	Residence	Qualified	Term
Richard Dobbs Spaight	Craven	January 6, 1795	1795
Samuel Ashe	New Hanover	November 19, 1795	1795-1796
Samuel Ashe	New Hanover	December 19, 1796	1796-1797
Samuel Ashe	New Hanover	December 5, 1797	1797-1798
William R. Davie	Halifax	December 7, 1798	1798-1799
Benjamin Williams	Moore	November 23, 1799	1799-1800
Benjamin Williams	Moore	November 29, 1800	1800-1801
Benjamin Williams	Moore	November 28, 1801	1801-1802
John Baptiste Ashe	Halifax	—	—
James Turner	Warren	December 6, 1802	1802-1803
James Turner	Warren	December 6, 1803	1803-1804
James Turner	Warren	November 24, 1804	1804-1805
Nathaniel Alexander	Mecklenburg	December 10, 1805	1805-1806
Nathaniel Alexander	Mecklenburg	December 1, 1806	1806-1807
Benjamin Williams	Moore	December 1, 1807	1807-1808
David Stone	Bertie	December 12, 1808	1808-1809
David Stone	Bertie	December 13, 1809	1809-1810
Benjamin Smith	Brunswick	December 5, 1810	1810-1811
William Hawkins	Warren	December 9, 1811	1811-1812
William Hawkins	Warren	December 8, 1812	1812-1813
William Hawkins	Warren	December 7, 1813	1813-1814
William Miller	Warren	December 7, 1814	1814-1815
William Miller	Warren	December 7, 1815	1815-1816
William Miller	Warren	December 7, 1816	1816-1817
John Branch	Halifax	December 6, 1817	1817-1818
John Branch	Halifax	December 5, 1818	1818-1819
John Branch	Halifax	December 7, 1819	1819-1820
Jesse Franklin	Surry	December 7, 1820	1820-1821
Gabriel Holmes	Sampson	December 7, 1821	1821-1822
Gabriel Holmes	Sampson	December 7, 1822	1822-1823
Gabriel Holmes	Sampson	December 6, 1823	1823-1824
Hutchings G. Burton	Halifax	December 7, 1824	1824-1825
Hutchings G. Burton	Halifax	December 6, 1825	1825-1826
Hutchings G. Burton	Halifax	December 29, 1826	1826-1827
James Iredell Jr.	Chowan	December 8, 1827	1827-1828
John Owen	Bladen	December 12, 1828	1828-1829
John Owen	Bladen	December 10, 1829	1829-1830
Montford Stokes	Wilkes	December 18, 1830	1830-1831
Montford Stokes	Wilkes	December 13, 1831	1831-1832
David L. Swain	Buncombe	December 6, 1832	1832-1833
David L. Swain	Buncombe	December 9, 1833	1833-1834
David L. Swain	Buncombe	December 10, 1834	1834-1835
Richard Dobbs Spaight Jr.	Craven	December 10, 1835	1835-1836

ELECTED BY THE PEOPLE—TWO-YEAR TERM

Name	Residence	Qualified	Term
Edward B. Dudley	New Hanover	December 31, 1836	1836-1838
Edward B. Dudley	New Hanover	December 29, 1838	1838-1841
John M. Morehead	Guilford	January 1, 1841	1841-1842
John M. Morehead	Guilford	December 31, 1842	1842-1845
William A. Graham	Orange	January 1, 1845	1845-1847
William A. Graham	Orange	January 1, 1847	1847-1849
Charles Manly	Wake	January 1, 1849	1849-1851
David S. Reid	Rockingham	January 1, 1851	1851-1852
David S. Reid	Rockingham	December 22, 1852	1852-1854
Warren Winslow	Cumberland	December 6, 1854	1854-1855
Thomas Bragg	Northampton	January 1, 1855	1855-1857
Thomas Bragg	Northampton	January 1, 1857	1857-1859
John W. Ellis	Rowan	January 1, 1859	1859-1861
John W. Ellis	Rowan	January 1, 1861	1861
Henry T. Clark	Edgecombe	July 7, 1861	1861-1862
Zebulon B. Vance	Buncombe	September 8, 1862	1862-1864
Zebulon B. Vance	Buncombe	December 22, 1864	1864-1865
William W. Holden	Wake	May 29, 1865	1865
Jonathan Worth	Randolph	December 15, 1865	1865-1866
Jonathan Worth	Randolph	December 22, 1866	1866-1868

ELECTED BY THE PEOPLE—FOUR-YEAR TERM

Name	Residence	Qualified	Term
William W. Holden	Wake	July 1, 1868	1868-1870
Tod R. Caldwell	Burke	December 15, 1870	1870-1873
Tod R. Caldwell	Burke	January 1, 1873	1873-1874
Curtis H. Brogden	Wayne	July 14, 1874	1874-1877
Zebulon B. Vance	Buncombe	January 1, 1877	1877-1879
Thomas J. Jarvis	Pitt	February 5, 1879	1879-1881
Thomas J. Jarvis	Pitt	January 18, 1881	1881-1885
James L. Robinson	Macon	September 1, 1883	1883
Alfred M. Scales	Rockingham	January 21, 1885	1885-1889
Daniel G. Fowle	Wake	January 17, 1889	1889-1891
Thomas M. Holt	Alamance	April 8, 1891	1891-1893
Elias Carr	Edgecombe	January 18, 1893	1893-1897
Daniel L. Russell	Brunswick	January 12, 1897	1897-1901
Charles B. Aycock	Wayne	January 15, 1901	1901-1905
Robert B. Glenn	Forsyth	January 11, 1905	1905-1909
William W. Kitchin	Person	January 12, 1909	1909-1913
Locke Craig	Buncombe	January 15, 1913	1913-1917
Thomas W. Bickett	Franklin	January 11, 1917	1917-1921
Cameron Morrison	Mecklenburg	January 12, 1921	1921-1925
Angus W. McLean	Robeson	January 14, 1925	1925-1929

Name	Residence	Qualified	Term
Oliver Max Gardner	Cleveland	January 11, 1929	1929-1933
John C. B. Ehringhaus	Pasquotank	January 5, 1933	1933-1937
Clyde R. Hoey	Cleveland	January 7, 1937	1937-1941
John Melville Broughton	Wake	January 9, 1941	1941-1945
Robert Gregg Cherry	Gaston	January 4, 1945	1945-1949
William Kerr Scott	Alamance	January 6, 1949	1949-1953
William B. Umstead	Durham	January 8, 1953	1953-1954
Luther H. Hodges	Rockingham	November 7, 1954	1954-1957
Luther H. Hodges	Rockingham	February 7, 1957	1957-1961
Terry Sanford	Cumberland	January 5, 1961	1961-1965
Daniel K. Moore	Jackson	January 8, 1965	1965-1969
Robert W. Scott	Alamance	January 3, 1969	1969-1973
James E. Holshouser Jr.	Watauga	January 5, 1973	1973-1977
James B. Hunt Jr.	Wilson	January 8, 1977	1977-1981
James B. Hunt Jr.	Wilson	January 10, 1981	1981-1985
James G. Martin	Iredell	January 5, 1985	1985-1989
James G. Martin	Iredell	January 7, 1989	1989-1993
James B. Hunt Jr.	Wilson	January 9, 1993	1993-1997
James B. Hunt Jr.	Wilson	January 11, 1997	1997-2001
Michael Francis Easley	Nash	January 6, 2001	2001-2005
Michael Francis Easley	Nash	January 15, 2005	2005-

INDEX

Page numbers in italics refer to illustrations.

Executive Mansion Fund, Inc., 37
Executive Residence. *See* Executive
  Mansion

F

Fair Bluff Watermelon Festival, 84
Festivals, 84, 85, 86, 87, 88-89, 90
Fifth Provincial Congress, 10, 43
Finley, A. E., 19
First ladies, 36, 38
Fish. *See* Freshwater trout, state;
  Saltwater fish, state
Flag, state, 49-53, 54; act promoting
  display of, 52; of 1861, 49, 50; of
  1885, 50-51, 52; modifications to,
  52; salute to, 53; use of, by North
  Carolina troops, 50
Flenniken, John, 54
Florida, 3, 75
Florida Gulf region, 1
Flower, state, *58, 59. See also*
  Wildflower, state
Folkmoot USA, 85
Food festival of Piedmont Triad
  region, official, 88-89
Ford, John, 54
Forsyth County, 94
Fort Fisher, 90
Fourth Provincial Congress, 7
Fowle, Daniel G., 27, 30, 94
France, 1
Francis I (king of France), 1
Franklin, Jesse, 93
Franklin County, 94
Fraser, John, 81
Fraser fir, 80-81
Freshwater trout, state, 82
Fruit, state, 73
Fundamental Constitutions of
  Carolina, 5. *See also* Colonial
  government

G

Gardner, Fay Lamar Webb
  (Mrs. O. Max Gardner), 32
Gardner, Oliver Max, 32, 95
Gaston, William Joseph, 57
Gaston County, 95
Gibbs, John, 91
Gill, Edwin, 19

Glenn, Robert B., 28, 94
Glover, William, 40, 91
Governor's Mansion. *See* Executive
  Mansion
Governor's Palace, 22, 23. *See also*
  Executive Mansion
Governor's Western Residence, 37,
  38. *See also* Executive Mansion
Graham, William (Mecklenburg
  Declaration signer), 54
Graham, William A. (governor), 16, 94
Granite, 67, *68*
Granville, Lord. *See* Carteret, John,
  Earl Granville
Granville Grant, *4*
Graves, Philmore, *86*
Great Seal, The, 39, 42-48, 54;
  General Assembly provides a
  standard for, 46
Great Smoky Mountains National
  Park, 85
Guilford County, 92, 94

H

Hakluyt, Richard, 1
Halifax, 7, 13, 42
Halifax County, 93
Halifax Resolution. *See* Halifax
  Resolves
Halifax Resolves, 7-9, 47, 52
Ham, Marie Sharpe, 35
Harris, James, 54
Harris, Richard, 54
Harvey, John, 91
Harvey, Thomas, 91
Hasell, James, 92
Hatteras, 1, 69
Hawkins, William, 93
Hertford County Watermelon
  Festival, 84
Hewes, Joseph, *8,* 9, 43
Hewlett, Addison, 19
Hicks, William J., 25, 26
Hiddenite. *See* Precious stone, state
Hill, James, 65. *See also* Precious
  stone, state
Hillsborough, 13
Hillsborough, Earl of, 42
Historical boat, state, 69
Hodges, Luther H., 19, 32, 95

"Mother Vineyard." *See* Scuppernong
  grape
Motto, state, 45, 47, 56
Mount Airy, 67, 68
Mount Mitchell, 56, 81
Muscadine grape. *See* Scuppernong
  grape
Museum of North Carolina
  Traditional Pottery, 86

N

Nags Head, *79*
Nash, Abner, 92
Nash, Atwood and, 31
Nash County, 95
Nature Conservancy, The, 76
New Bern, 11, 13, 41, 57
New Hanover County, 22, 93, 94
New York, 64
News and Observer (Raleigh), 25
Nichols, William (architect, father), 13
Nichols, William, Jr. (architect, son), 13
Nicknames, state: Old North State,
  The, 3, 56, 57; Tar Heel State, The, 3
North Carolina Aviation Hall of
  Fame, 85
North Carolina Aviation Museum, 85
North Carolina Museum of Aviation,
  85
North Carolina Pottery Center, 86
Northampton County, 94

O

Oak Ridge, 83
Oak Ridge Military Academy, 83
Ogilby Map, *viii*
Orange County, 92, 94
Orange Street ArtsFest, 90
Oregon, 80
Owen, John, 93

P

Pamlico County, 75
Pasquotank County, 95
Paton, David, 13, 14, 25
Patton, Benjamin, 54
Pearce, Lorraine, 33
Penn, John, *8*, 9
Person County, 94
Pettigrew Hospital, 26

Phifer, John, 54
Philadelphia, 9, 15, 32, 44, 52
Pick-Your-Own farms: how to find, 74
Piedmont Triad region, 88
Pier-Giavina, H., 31
Pine, *60*, 61
Pine, long leaf, 56
Pitt County, 87, 94
Plott, Johannes George, 70
Plott hound, 70
Polk, Thomas, 54
Pollock, Thomas, 91, 92
Pottery and potters, 85-86
Precious stone, state, 64, 65
Products: brick, 36; heart pine, 35-36;
  pitch (resin), 3, 61; tar, 3, 61; textile,
  36; turpentine, 3, 61; wood, 61
Proprietors, Lords. *See* Lords
  Proprietors

Q

Quakers. *See* Society of Friends
Quary, John, 54

R

Raleigh, Sir Walter, 1, 21, 73
Raleigh: artisans from, 16, 49; capital
  established in, 11, 13, 21; mentioned,
  12, 14, 18, 23, 26, 35, 78
Randolph County, 85, 94
Ransom, Matthew W., 16
Rebel Council, 91
Red drum. *See* Channel bass
Reed, William, 92
Reese, David, 54
Reeves, Ralph B., Jr., 19
Reid, David S., 94
Reptile, state, 66
Revolutionary War, 7, 44;
  Continental Congress meets prior
  to, 7, 9; Declaration of
  Independence signed prior to, 8, 9
Rice, Nathaniel, 92
Roanoke Island, 1, 69, 73
Robeson County, 94
Robinson, James L., 94
Rock, state, 67, 68
Rockingham County, 94, 95
Rollos (chief engraver of seals), 41
Rowan, Matthew, 92